LANDS' END® BUSINESS ATTIRE FOR WOMEN

LANDS' END
BUSINESS ATTIRE FOR
WOMEN
MASTERING THE NEW ABCs
OF WHAT TO WEAR TO WORK

LANDS' END

TEXT BY TODD LYON

CLARKSON POTTER/ PUBLISHERS
NEW YORK

A Stonesong Press Book
Published by Clarkson Potter/Publishers, New York, New York
Member of the Crown Publishing Group, a division of Random House, Inc.
www.crownpublishing.com

CLARKSON N. POTTER is a trademark and POTTER and colophon are registered trademarks of Random House, Inc.

Printed in Singapore

Design by Blue Cup Creative, Inc./Wayne Wolf

Illustrations by Rachael Phillips
Diagrams on page 104 by chrisorr.com

Library of Congress Cataloging-in-Publication Data
Lands' End business attire for women: mastering the new ABCs of what to wear to work /
Lands' End ; text by Todd Lyon.
       p.   cm.
1. Clothing and dress.   2. Fashion.   I. Lyon, Todd.   II. Lands' End, Inc.   III. Title.
    TT507.L25   2004
    646'.34–dc21   2003013633

ISBN 0-609-61019-8

10   9   8   7   6   5   4   3   2   1

First Edition

This book is dedicated to Susan Gray Lichtenstein (1935–1996), my longtime publisher, friend, and style guru. Sue imparted much wisdom to me over the years, but the lesson I remembered best happened on her sixtieth birthday, when I asked her how she managed to stay so chic. She pondered my question for a long moment—this widowed mother of two, this former model and ardent gardener, with her cropped gray hair, arched eyebrows, perfect earrings, flattering outfit, and soft shoes planted sweetly below crossed ankles—then replied, "You have to shop. A lot."

It was no small statement. She had been shopping all her life. Not only for great clothes, but also for places to live, schools for her sons, men to pursue, plays to see, classes to take, friends to cultivate, and, especially, projects that would fulfill her, emotionally and financially.

Sue was an adventurous woman who didn't wait for life to blunder up her steps and ring her bell. She went out and explored her options, then made choices. Became an expert skier. Dated an astronaut. Bicycled through Europe. Bought important art. Launched a monthly newspaper. Won national awards.

Sue shopped. What she didn't find in the marketplace, she created herself, and ultimately she shared her passions—and her stunning personal style—with thousands of lucky people, including me.

Here's to the memory of the beautiful Ms. Lichtenstein, and to the power of profound shopping.

—T.L.

ACKNOWLEDGMENTS

My heartfelt thanks go to Ellen Scordato at Stonesong Press, who masterminded this book, proved to have impeccable taste in clothing, and was an excellent travel mate and quite patient while my shoes were being scanned in airports.

Shout-outs also go to Colleen Mohyde, my intrepid agent, and Katie Workman, my favorite editor in the whole wide world.

Finally, I'd like to thank the good-hearted folks at Lands' End, who fuss over every button, seam, and hem so that you won't have to.

—T.L.

CONTENTS

INTRODUCTION: WHAT IS BUSINESS CASUAL?

For much of the twentieth century,

the average American "career gal" didn't dream of heading to the office without a proper hat and gloves, no matter what the season. Though she might remove them before getting down to business—witness Rosalind Russell playing a star reporter in *His Girl Friday* (1940)—she was expected to conform to a complex and fairly inflexible set of standards that dictated the length of her skirt, the height of her heels, the color of her stockings, and much more.

Today, a flip through television channels will reveal images of working women in a host of wildly differing styles: a young lawyer arguing cases in a thigh-high miniskirt *(Ally McBeal)*; a successful newspaper columnist running around in hot pants, spike heels, and a poncho *(Sex and the City)*; a real-life multimillionaire baking pies in a casual, comfortable sweater *(From Martha's Kitchen)*; and a middle-aged Englishwoman running a company in pink tights and platform shoes *(Absolutely Fabulous)*.

In the real world, of course, business fashions are rarely so eccentric. But the fact remains that women's roles in the workplace have evolved at a breathtaking pace—and business attire has followed closely behind.

As far back as the 1860s, the few female office workers wore feminized versions of men's suits—at that time, ankle-length skirts, high-neck blouses, and button-front jackets. When World War I broke out in 1914, large numbers of women took factory jobs to help the war effort but many continued to wear their sometimes cumbersome skirts and long tresses, looking askance at sheared hair and calf-length hemlines. The changing mores and fashions of the 1920s and '30s revolutionized women's work wear: Skirts rose above the ankles, arms were bared, corsets and bustles disappeared, and even the pope decreed that short hair was not a mark of immorality.

During World War II, government rationing had a profound impact on the fashions of the day. Silk stockings were rare, dress lengths climbed to the knee, ruffles were banished, and the pencil skirt—cut in a straight line from hips to hem—became popular. As women filled manufacturing jobs to replace the men who had gone to war, pants became slightly more

What did working women wear in the first half of the twentieth century? You might be surprised! *From left to right:* A 1920s Jazz Age secretary in Washington, D.C., shows off her fashionable soft Russian boots and the latest bobbed hair. A patriotic female factory worker during World War II models a futuristic yet practical jumpsuit. A prosperous working woman greets the 1950s in a New Look dress with an exuberant polka-dot pattern.

acceptable, and the image of Rosie the Riveter, in her work uniform, was especially influential.

After the war, feminine styles came rushing back into homes and offices, led by Christian Dior's New Look, which exaggerated the female form with nipped waists and flaring skirts. In 1959, the Mattel toy company released a Commuter Barbie doll, dressed in a modest Chanel-type suit and hat, open-toed pumps, and tiny white gloves—a look very popular among women office workers.

By the 1970s, large numbers of women began infiltrating the rarefied ranks of male executives. One of their weapons involved "dressing for success"—which meant, very often, adopting and adapting men's business fashions. Though the massive shoulder pads and modified neckties of the 1980s look outdated now, the modern woman's basic business style remained fairly stable for nearly thirty years, centered around blazers, blouses, tailored pants, and modest skirts.

Then came "business casual" dress codes. The crisp division between work clothes and play clothes was blurred. Women's closets became battle zones where sweater sets rebelled against structured jackets, easy chinos challenged wool trousers, and comfy flats threatened to render pumps extinct.

The change took root in the 1990s, as the Information Age dawned. While anchorwomen, upper-management professionals, and

elected officials continued to follow clear and rather stringent codes of dress, other professional women faced brand-new choices. Increasingly decentralized offices and the telecommunications revolution were shrinking some offices down to the size of a laptop and a cell phone, which made "dressing for work" a confusing concept. Toward the end of the decade, a hiring crunch inspired many human resources departments to lure talented women and men via "dress down" policies that allowed staffers to be more comfortable and, allegedly, more productive.

Now that huge numbers of corporations, large and small, have adopted full-time casual dress codes, two main problems have crystallized. The first is that many hardworking women (and men) have sabotaged their careers by misinterpreting the new rules and dressing inappropriately. The second is that the economic landscape continues to change, currently prompting a general shift away from ultra-relaxed modes.

"Business casual" may sound like an oxymoron, but it is a standard of dress that millions of employees seek to achieve on a daily basis. Within this new reality, women of style have a unique challenge: They need to be comfortable and look professional, while avoiding the risk of appearing provocative or overly trendy in the office.

It's no wonder that so many women puzzle through their closets every morning, trying to find pieces that will fit together and form the right look for the day's challenges. Can you go to work in an oxford shirt and chinos? Will you be taken seriously in a delicate cardigan and a flowing skirt? How about in bell-bottoms and high-heeled boots? If it's true that "conservative" is perceived as "responsible," should you opt for a classic ensemble that nods to old-school traditional while incorporating elements of new-world casual? Or should you just wear your favorite jeans and carry a blazer, in case you're called into a meeting?

Business casual needn't be a burden, nor should it cause confusion. With the right image in mind and the right clothing on your shopping list, you can create a system of dressing that not only saves you time and money, but also expresses your ambitions and your sense of style. Step by step, piece by piece, this book will guide you through a jumble of options and help you build a working wardrobe that is appropriate, flexible, and flattering.

Top
10
Casual Mistakes for Women

1. Too-comfortable clothing better suited for sports or weekend wear (sweatshirts, sweatpants, rumpled chinos, oversized shirts, running shoes, etc.)

2. Jeans (except neat, conservative jeans on designated days or when appropriate)

3. T-shirts (unless layered under a jacket or sweater)

4. Clothing that reveals too much (low-cut tops, cropped tops, translucent shirts, very tight clothes, miniskirts, etc.)

5. Elements more appropriate for evening (heavy makeup, shiny or glittery fabrics, fishnets, very high heels, etc.)

6. Clothing with slogans, logos, or prominent brand names

7. Ultra-trendy or costumey outfits, accessories, and/or jewelry

8. Dowdy, worn-out clothes and shoes

9. Clothes that don't fit and/or don't flatter

10. Too many accessories

SHIRT
Stretch cotton
shirt, French blue

JEWELRY
Single-strand pearl necklace,
pearl earrings

JACKET
Classic blazer, black

SKIRT
Skirt with inverted
pleats, black

SHOES
Classic leather pumps, black

TRADITIONAL BUSINESS ATTIRE

When crucial business is being conducted, men reach for their most conservative suits. Presidents, congressmen, candidates, kings . . . they know that, all over the world, the dark suit is a symbol of power and professionalism.

Same goes for women.

Based on classic men's suiting, the über-traditional ensemble for businesswomen is a structured, skirted suit in sober tones. The tailored blazer tends to hide feminine curves, yet the mid-calf skirt, worn with modest pumps, nods to the old-fashioned concept of skirts being "ladylike."

Shown here with a collared shirt and pearls, the traditional suit may also be worn with a soft blouse or accessorized with a scarf. But it is not a vehicle for self-expression, nor is it designed with comfort in mind. Rather, it is a uniform that identifies the wearer as an established professional who, no doubt, works within a culture of old-school formalities.

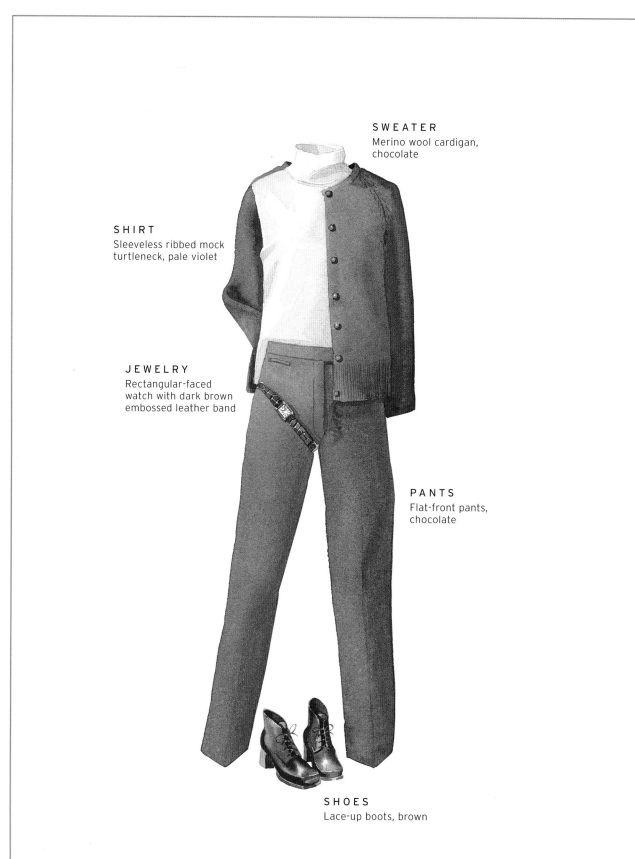

SWEATER
Merino wool cardigan,
chocolate

SHIRT
Sleeveless ribbed mock
turtleneck, pale violet

JEWELRY
Rectangular-faced
watch with dark brown
embossed leather band

PANTS
Flat-front pants,
chocolate

SHOES
Lace-up boots, brown

BUSINESS CASUAL ATTIRE

The look is coordinated, attractive, unfussy. It may not be acceptable at an international summit at the White House, but it's certainly appropriate for day-to-day operations at any office or place of business that isn't strictly formal.

Here, the business suit concept has evolved into an outfit that is comfortable and practical. The structured blazer has been replaced by a supple cardigan sweater, and the stiff shirt has been traded for a soft, sleeveless turtleneck. Instead of a stern wool skirt, this ensemble features flexible trousers that enable you to run for a taxi, climb a step stool for a stored file, and give a presentation to the sales staff, looking great all the while.

Like the traditional suit, the business casual ensemble relies on coordinated colors, sympathetic fabrics, and an overall sense of simplicity to ensure a professional look. And although high-heeled boots add style and the sweaters may be touchably soft, the outfit doesn't emphasize the female figure.

In many ways, business casual is just as conservative as traditional business attire. It has a number of advantages, however. For instance, you'll save on dry-cleaning bills, you can choose from a broader range of styles, your feet won't hurt, you'll stay cooler in the summer and warmer in the winter, and you won't desperately peel off your clothes the minute you get home from work.

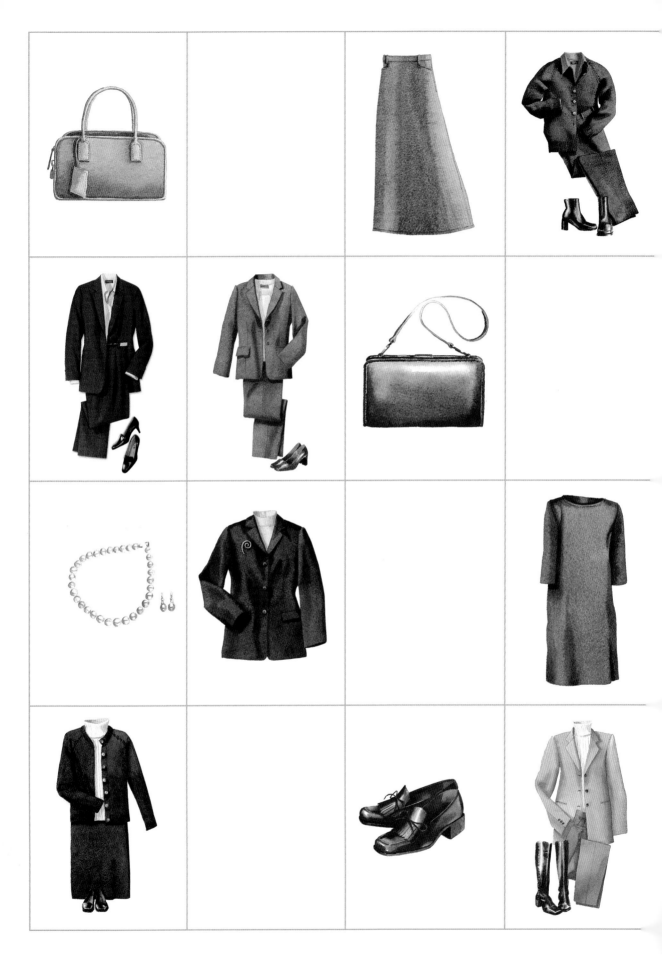

1

DETERMINING YOUR LEVEL OF BUSINESS CASUAL

Business casual isn't an exact science.

An art director can wear simple slacks and flats when working with photographers and writers, then don chic designer suits for meetings with editors, publishers, or advertisers. A regional director of a nonprofit agency can get by in polo shirts and chinos all day, then turn polished and professional when hobnobbing with potential benefactors. One woman, for example, who runs a small architectural firm, often finds herself visiting construction sites, meeting with clients, and working on blueprints all in a single day. She keeps a dressy blazer, a weatherproof field coat, and a sturdy pair of boots in her office in order to meet her ever-changing needs.

Though some women can adopt a standard business uniform that serves them well Monday through Friday, there are many more who require a tremendous amount of flexibility. Virtually every woman, however, has a baseline level of business casual that informs her working wardrobe. Once you identify your business casual archetype, getting dressed in the morning becomes much, much easier.

So, where do you fit in? There are a few ways to find out. First, you should check your company's official dress code. Though it might not

SWEATER
Relaxed cotton
crewneck, light blue

JACKET
Classic gabardine blazer,
three-button, light gray

PANTS
Classic gabardine
pants, pleated
front, light gray

SHIRT
Broadcloth shirt, light
blue

PANTS
Stretch-knit pants,
flat front, white

SHOES
Loafers, black leather

help you become a fashion plate, it will at least identify items of clothing that you *shouldn't* wear. Second, look at how your coworkers dress, to see how they've interpreted the business casual mode. Although it can be misleading to use your peers as a guide, there might be one or two colleagues who look appropriately stylish and whom you may want to emulate. Which raises the question: Assuming you don't have a private dressing room in your office, is it possible to put together outfits, day after day, that meet the challenges that crop up from nine to five and beyond?

Finally, take the following visual quiz. Look at the four outfits presented and rate them in relation to your needs.

The
BUSINESS CASUAL
QUIZ

Is your pencil sharpened? Is your mind clear? Excellent. You're ready to be tested on your level of business casual.

INSTRUCTIONS

Look at the four outfits pictured on the following pages.

✳

Imagine that each outfit has magically appeared in your closet and fits you perfectly.

✳

Using the multiple-choice options, rate the outfits in relation to your current business needs.

✳

Be aware that there are no "right" or "wrong" answers.

✳

The Business Casual Quiz is based on your honest assessment of your occupation and working environment.

✳

Finally, turn to "The Results and How to Interpret Them," on page 29.

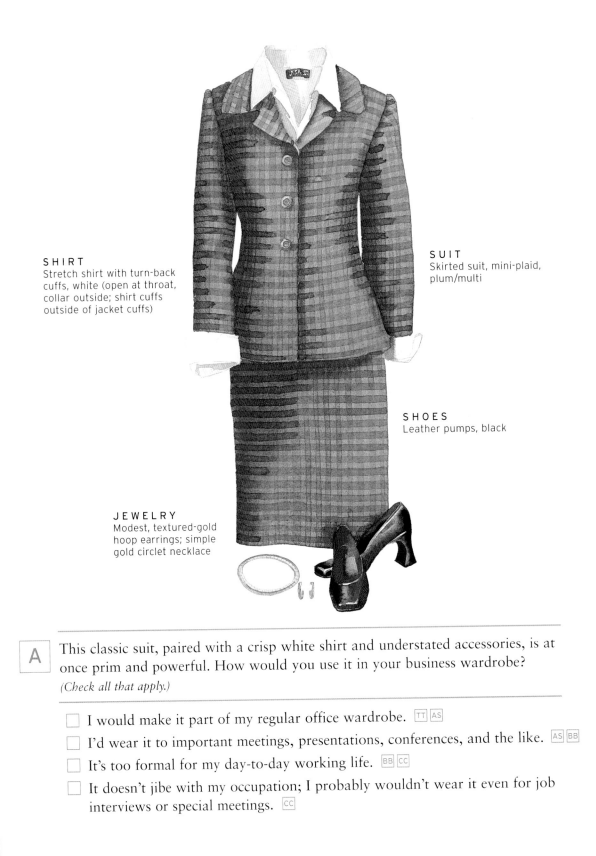

SHIRT
Stretch shirt with turn-back cuffs, white (open at throat, collar outside; shirt cuffs outside of jacket cuffs)

SUIT
Skirted suit, mini-plaid, plum/multi

SHOES
Leather pumps, black

JEWELRY
Modest, textured-gold hoop earrings; simple gold circlet necklace

---

A This classic suit, paired with a crisp white shirt and understated accessories, is at once prim and powerful. How would you use it in your business wardrobe?
(Check all that apply.)

☐ I would make it part of my regular office wardrobe. TT AS

☐ I'd wear it to important meetings, presentations, conferences, and the like. AS BB

☐ It's too formal for my day-to-day working life. BB CC

☐ It doesn't jibe with my occupation; I probably wouldn't wear it even for job interviews or special meetings. CC

JACKET
Jacket with gold buttons, multicolored

SHIRT
Stretch shirt, pale green

SKIRT
Long knit skirt, vintage green

BELT
Belt with circular gold buckle, brown

SCARF
Silk scarf, orange, gold, and green

SHOES
Two-piece pumps, brown

JEWELRY
Gold tab earrings

B A flowing knit skirt, a coordinating shirt, and an unstructured, multihued jacket form the base of this outfit; it's accessorized with strappy brown shoes and a matching belt, a colorful scarf, and simple gold earrings. How would you put this ensemble to work? *(Check all that apply.)*

- ☐ I'd wear it only on designated casual days. `TT`
- ☐ I'd take it out for major events at the office. `AS` `BB` `CC`
- ☐ It would become part of my regular working wardrobe. `AS` `BB`
- ☐ I'd probably save it for my private life; it's too fancy for my workplace. `CC`

SWEATERS
Tipped twinset, red
with black trim

PANTS
Plain-front gabardine
trousers, black

SHOES
Short leather boots,
black

JEWELRY
Classic watch,
black on black

C Plain-front gabardine trousers, groovy boots, and a cozy red twinset . . . relaxed,
yet stylish (especially with the addition of a chic wristwatch). What would you
do with this outfit, on the job? *(Check all that apply.)*

☐ I'd wear it to important meetings, conferences, and the like. BB CC

☐ I might wear it out to dinner, but not to work—it's too dressy. CC

☐ I'd make good use of it in my day-to-day working wardrobe. AS BB

☐ I'd reserve it for designated casual days. TT AS

SWEATER
Cotton Drifter
turtleneck, lilac

PANTS
Flat-front contour chinos,
field khaki

SHOES
Brazilian driving mocs,
brown

D   Comfort is a luxury. Example: easy chinos plus a cotton-knit sweater and a pair of flat, forgiving mocs. How would this laid-back formula fit into your professional life? *(Check all that apply.)*

☐ Just my style; I usually go to work in clothes like these. `CC`

☐ I'd dare to wear this outfit only on designated casual days. `AS` `BB`

☐ Unfortunately, it's too casual even for casual days. `TT`

☐ I'd probably take elements of this outfit and pair them with dressier pieces. `AS` `BB`

SCORING

Look at each answer that you checked off. To the right of each answer are one or more coded initials: TT, AS, BB, CC. Tally up these initials and mark the totals below.

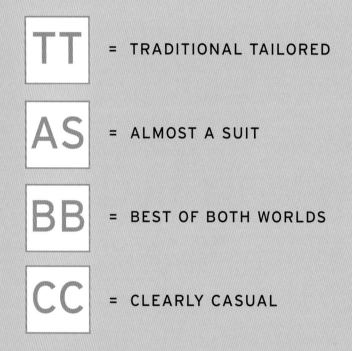

TT = TRADITIONAL TAILORED

AS = ALMOST A SUIT

BB = BEST OF BOTH WORLDS

CC = CLEARLY CASUAL

The category in which you scored the most points indicates the general level of business casual. This knowledge will help steer you toward creating a wardrobe that's right for you, your job, and your place of business.

THE RESULTS AND HOW TO INTERPRET THEM

DEFINING THE ARCHETYPES

If you scored highest in the Traditional Tailored (TT) category, you probably work in a traditional office and have adopted a profession in which dignity, reliability, and old-fashioned values are signaled via sober suits and modest pumps. Sometimes buttoned-up professionals like yourself are most baffled when their employers suddenly institute casual days.

If you scored highest in the Almost a Suit (AS) category, your place of business is professional but not bound by old-world traditions or protocol. In AS environments, conservative blazers, tops, and trousers are perfectly acceptable, as are modest skirts, dresses, and pumps.

If you scored highest in the Best of Both Worlds (BB) category, you likely have a number of on-the-job roles that call for a laid-back look on some days and a businesslike ensemble on others. BB is the most flexible category of business casual, and outfits range from chinos and a sweater to a skirted suit.

If you scored highest in the Clearly Casual (CC) category, chances are you work with your body as well as your mind, or your job requires little or no public contact. CC types rarely have a need for traditional business attire, but they do need to be comfortable while looking neat, coordinated, and appropriate.

TT

BLAZER
Classic wool blazer,
navy

SHIRT
Stretch cotton
blouse, white

SCARF
Silk chiffon scarf,
blue

SKIRT
Classic no-waistband
mid-calf wool skirt,
navy

YOU MIGHT BE A "TT" TYPE IF YOU

* work in banking, law, politics, finance, or insurance
* have an impressive position (president, CEO, CFO, COO, chairperson, anchor-woman, diplomat, elected official, founder, owner, partner, director, judge, attorney, publisher, editor in chief, superintendent, chancellor)
* recruit valuable assets for your firm
* regularly give press conferences or keynote addresses
* have something expensive to sell (cruise ships, commercial property, manufacturing contracts)
* represent your company overseas or to foreign clients
* often meet with TT clients or colleagues

AS

SWEATER
Turtleneck, camel

SCARF
Paisley chiffon scarf,
camel/blue

BLAZER
Single-button
gabardine blazer,
gray

PANTS
Pleated gabardine
trousers, gray

YOU MIGHT BE AN "AS" TYPE IF YOU

* work in publishing, marketing, human resources, sales, real estate, high-end retail, or education
* have a directorial or managerial position in a large corporation that has relaxed its dress codes over the years
* regularly meet with semicasual clients and/or colleagues
* are an executive at a semicasual company

SHIRT
Broadcloth shirt,
light blue

BELT
Leather, dark brown

BLAZER
Two-button blazer,
slate blue

PANTS
Pleated tailored
twills, cream

YOU MIGHT BE A "BB" TYPE IF YOU

* work in engineering, manufacturing, academia, health care, social services, tourism, or creative industries such as music, film, graphics, catering, or entertainment
* travel extensively on business and need to look professional, yet still be comfortable

* work in a creative department of a corporation
* work at home and go out for meetings and conferences
* are a freelancer
* head a two- or three-person company
* are a principal at a casual firm

CC

SWEATER
Cowl-neck sweater,
gray cotton

PANTS
Stretch-knit pants,
light gray

YOU MIGHT BE A "CC" TYPE IF YOU

* are a technician, code writer, or other expert who has more contact with machines than with humans
* work in a laboratory
* work at an Internet company, especially if it was started by people in their twenties

* are involved strictly in "back of house" operations
* are often physically active on the job (bartender, decorator, nurse, stylist, physical therapist, photographer)
* are employed by a laid-back firm where every day is a casual day

WHAT'S NEXT?

Have you zeroed in on your business casual archetype? Excellent. Your next assignment is to read this book and pay special attention to the outfits and outlines that relate to you and your particular situation.

Not everybody fits neatly into a single category, however.

If you are on the cusp of two or more categories (that is, if your test has resulted in a tied score between archetypes, or if there is a slim margin between your highest-scoring categories), your wardrobe demands are broader than average and call for creative solutions. If, for instance, you have nearly as many points in the Traditional Tailored category as in the Clearly Casual category, you'll need a closetful of comfortable, easy-care ensembles as well as an arsenal of classic trousers, skirts, and blazers.

Those of you whose scores straddle Almost a Suit, Best of Both Worlds, and/or Clearly Casual have an easier time of it: Once you understand the essential pieces in each of those categories, it's fairly easy to intensify your level of dressiness or dial it down, as needed.

Now it's time to break the news: Only three of the four types—Almost a Suit, Best of Both Worlds, and Clearly Casual—are addressed in this book. These categories apply to the majority of Americans who have to contend with casual dress codes at their place of work. But even if your test results are outside the assigned parameters, you can benefit from knowing the nuances of business casual dressing.

If you've tested as a Traditional Tailored type, and are confronted with casual days at the office, study the Almost a Suit entries for guidance.

SWEATERS
Twinset, yellow

SEPARATES
Classic gabardine
jacket and pants,
stone

SHOES
Loafers, black leather

ADVICE

FOR INTERNS, RECENT COLLEGE GRADS, AND ENTRY-LEVEL EMPLOYEES

If you're still in school, or freshly launched from the halls of academia into the cubicles of commerce, the rules of business casual dressing will bend for you . . . to a point. Many corporations allow a certain amount of latitude to their newest employees. It is understood that the young, lower-paid—and, in some cases, unpaid—members of the staff are in the midst of a stylistic transition. It isn't easy to go from classrooms to conference rooms, and everybody who was ever your age, even formidable CEOs, understands this. So, when avant-garde artists become administrative assistants, when club-goers turn into receptionists, and when German majors are hired as gofers, there is usually an unspecified (and largely implied) grace period in which the junior staffer in question is allowed to develop her business casual wardrobe.

With that said, please understand that if you are an entry-level employee—just out of school, or not—and you want to earn wages that put you above the poverty line, it's a good idea to dress like a grown-up. This doesn't mean you have to squelch your spirit. But if you study the corporate culture of your workplace and figure out a way to look responsible and appropriate (while maintaining your personal style and not breaking the bank, of course), you're more likely to gain the trust of your superiors and convince them that you're worthy of promotions, raises, and, when the time comes, solid recommendations to future employers.

Your mission, should you decide to accept it, is threefold. First, identify your current business casual archetype by taking the quiz on page 23. Then, comb through your existing wardrobe and assemble the pieces that could work in your professional environment. Finally, identify any basic elements that you're missing, and acquire them as best you can. Luckily, there are now more retail options than ever for shopping for flexible and timeless basics that can help form the foundation of a chic work wardrobe.

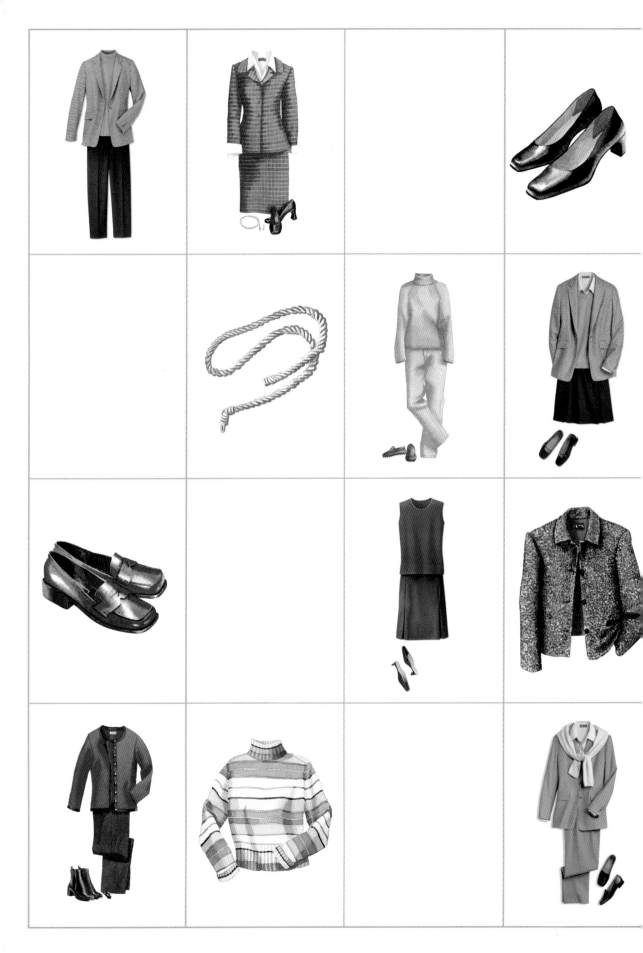

2

THE LOOKS THAT WORK

A BUSINESS CASUAL PRIMER

Are you aware that within thirty

seconds of meeting someone, you subconsciously rate his or her socio-economic status, educational level, and desirability? It's true. And you are rated the same way. Part of the snap judgment is based on what an individual says and how it's said, but most of it—55 percent, according to various scientific studies—is in direct relation to how the person looks.

Clothing is both a powerful communicator and an important business tool. Though judgment via fashion might seem unfair, in fact it presents a wonderful opportunity. By dressing to reflect your career objectives, you can send potent messages about your team spirit, ambition, creativity, and professionalism.

The ultimate goal is to set yourself up with essential articles of clothing that speak volumes about who you are, where you are, and where you're going. If you've taken Chapter 1 to heart, you already have a strong idea of your best professional look. Following is a basic overview of pieces that can further define each of the three business casual archetypes.

ALMOST A SUIT ENSEMBLES
Power Meets Personality

JACKET
Stretch gabardine blazer, cardinal

SHIRT
Long-sleeved stretch shirt, white

JACKET
Long three-button blazer, heathered taupe

SWEATER
Ribbed turtleneck, heather oatmeal

SKIRT
Wool skirt, red plaid

PANTS
Wool crepe trousers, tobacco

SHOES
Pumps, black

SHOES
Tall leather boots, chocolate

Bright colors can reflect beautifully on you. In the AS category, however, vivid hues work best in classic shapes. This skirted suit, for example, would be very conservative in navy or black. It's the red of the blazer and the lively plaid of the skirt that lift this outfit out of the Traditional Tailored category and into the slightly more casual, and definitely more interesting, realm of Almost a Suit.

Yes, you can take a pair of trousers, add a sweater, top them with a blazer, and look as if you're wearing a designer suit. The key? Related tones. There is very little contrast in this AS grouping. The jacket is heathered taupe, the sweater is oatmeal, the trousers are tobacco-colored, and the boots are chocolate brown, which echoes the jacket buttons. The result is a top-to-toe ensemble that doesn't look pieced together.

JACKET
Rayon/linen
blazer, dark navy

SWEATER
Short-sleeved sweater,
light cornflower

SWEATER
Ribbed turtleneck,
heather oatmeal

CARDIGAN
Cotton/rayon cardigan,
black

PANTS
Tropical-weight-
wool trousers,
navy

SHOES
Perforated pumps,
navy

SKIRT
Short wool skirt,
black

SHOES
Pumps, black

Navy is known as an old-guard color. But in the form of a linen pantsuit worn with pumps and enlivened by a cornflower-hued sweater, navy loses its severity and becomes . . . blue. It's charming, yet once again, a monochromatic scheme makes this outfit strong as well as chic. In fact, a brooch on the lapel or a scarf at the neck wouldn't undermine its authority.

A ribbed turtleneck . . . a soft-shouldered cardigan with prominent buttons . . . this outfit could be dangerously casual, if it weren't for the smart wool skirt and leather pumps snapping it right back into Almost a Suit land. Paired with the black skirt, the cardigan—also black—reads as a coordinating jacket, of sorts. Can you imagine the same cardigan in lavender, with chinos instead of a skirt? That would be Clearly Casual. This is not.

BEST OF BOTH WORLDS BLENDINGS
Miles of Versatile Style

SHOES
Tall leather boots,
chocolate with white
topstitching

SHIRT
Supima cotton
T-shirt, white

SWEATER
Cashmere cardigan,
light tan heather

SKIRT
Flannel skirt with
fringed hem, brown

JACKET
Wool flannel
zip-front blazer, black

SHIRT
Long-sleeved
stretch shirt, white

PANTS
Slim pants, black
plaid

SHOES
Oblique-toed
loafers, black

At first glance, it's a brown skirt with matching boots and a soft sweater set. Look more closely, and you'll note that the skirt is flannel, with a fringed hem, and under that cashmere cardigan is a cotton T-shirt. Casual and not-so-casual elements come together to create a perfectly appropriate (and quite fetching) look; that's what Best of Both Worlds is all about.

BB types can do variations on all sorts of themes. Here, the pantsuit is reinterpreted with a zip-front blazer and slim-cut plaid pants. Square-toed loafers and a classic white shirt pull it all together. In the business casual world, an outfit like this can go anywhere; think of it as an all-access pass.

SWEATER
Cotton/rayon
cardigan, black

SHIRT
Snap-front stretch
shirt, dark periwinkle

JACKET
Stretch gabardine
blazer, cardinal

SHIRT
Striped Supima cotton
tee, coral/poppy red

PANTS
Flat-front contour
chinos, black

SKIRT
Short skirt, black

SHOES
Leather boots, black

SHOES
Woven penny loafers,
black

Once again, the pantsuit is personalized. This time, a fingertip-length cardigan meets black chinos and ankle boots, while a periwinkle-blue shirt shows its cuffs and collar. It's easy to wear and easy to care for: Everything but the boots can be thrown in the washing machine.

Remember the traditional skirted suit? Here's the BB version. Though its familiar silhouette is intact, its upright reputation is loosened by a red blazer, a black skirt, a striped cotton T-shirt, and woven penny loafers. Remove the jacket and add a chunky belt for extra casual impact.

CLEARLY CASUAL COMBOS
All This and Comfy, Too

SWEATER
Notch-collar cardigan,
gray heather

SHIRT
Ballet-neck top with
stripes, black

PANTS
Flat-front contour
chinos, black

SHOES
Leather boots,
black

SWEATER
Ribbed turtleneck,
heather oatmeal

SHIRT
Suede big shirt,
chocolate

PANTS
Wool crepe
trousers, tobacco

SHOES
Box leather loafers,
brown

In Clearly Casual situations, you can wear clothes that are as cozy as pajamas. The challenge is to make them look not only presentable, but also professional. Example: This gray jacket that looks like a blazer is actually a cardigan, layered over a striped cotton jersey and flat-front chinos. You may be tempted to wear bedroom slippers with it, but don't: Real shoes (or shiny leather boots) will add panache and the aforementioned professional look.

The suede "big shirt" is unconstricting and drapes like a dream. Wear it over soft trousers, add a sweater and loafers, and voilà! Sharp style meets casual comfort. Note: For an even more casual look, try a big shirt in corduroy. Please avoid plaid flannel big shirts, however.

SWEATER
Turtleneck tunic
sweater, brick

PANTS
Slim pants, black
plaid

SHOES
Woven penny loafers,
black

SWEATER
Short-sleeve sweater,
light cornflower

CARDIGAN
Cashmere crewneck
cardigan, light tan
heather (tied around
shoulders)

PANTS
Side-zip twill
pants, light stone

SHOES
Brazilian driving mocs,
tan suede

A long, oversized sweater over slim pants is an easy solution for the CC workplace. Here, you see plaid pants and a brick-colored sweater, but virtually any combination—dark pants plus bright sweater, pale pants plus dark sweater, or matching pants and sweater—can also work well. *Note:* Slim pants are not the same as stretch pants or leggings, which are not acceptable in the workplace.

A waist-length sweater worn with simple trousers is also a good option for the Clearly Casual woman. Whenever you're tempted to wear a T-shirt or jersey to work, opt instead for a sweater, be it fine-gauge cashmere or chunky cable knit. Long-sleeved, short-sleeved, or sleeveless, a sweater always looks better than a common cotton jersey or tee.

ALL ABOUT
COLOR

Most women have an excellent sense of color and know instinctively which shades look good on them and which colors coordinate well with one another. Yet even experts might benefit from a few directional signals on the color wheel.

Black, brown, navy, gray, maroon, plum, and other dark colors are associated with autumn and winter.

White, off-white, and pastel colors are associated with the spring and summer months. Traditionally, any and all white or pastel shoes, purses, pants, and skirts are put away after Labor Day and brought out again after Memorial Day. This rule is no longer cast in stone, however, and is routinely ignored in southern states. Even in places that are snowed in from November to April, women of style wear "winter white" and related pastels. The success of this strategy depends on the fabrics, however. When the weather outside is frightful, it's perfectly okay to wear a pale lilac pashmina shawl, a blush-colored wool suit, or a cuddly sweater in celery green. But don't try to squeak by with summery pieces like a flowery cotton skirt or a white linen dress.

Dark colors, especially black, are preferred by big-city women in northern regions, no matter what the season. True anecdote: Last spring, a woman from Florida went to visit some friends in Manhattan. On her first day in the city, she put on her favorite white blouse, a powder-blue miniskirt, and white sandals. Then she got on the subway and found herself surrounded by women and men all dressed in black. "I looked like Rebecca of Sunnybrook Farm," she recalls. "It was as if I were glowing. I felt like I was wearing a big neon sign that said 'tourist.'" Lesson: When in major metropolitan areas, go for a dark, minimalist look if you have any interest in blending in.

In general, dark colors are considered dressier—or at least more serious and sober—than bright or light colors. One exception is red, which is perceived as a "power" color.

Neutral shades can be worn just about anytime, anywhere. Today's neutrals include shades of cream and beige; khaki; navy blue; gray; black; and most browns. White and off-white shirts, blouses, and tops are considered appropriate in any season. Neutrals can be a good choice for basic pieces such as skirts. A variety of skirt styles and lengths in a

few neutral shades form a solid foundation that you can wear year-round. You may play adventurously by adding colorful shoes, scarves, belts, and bags depending on the season, and choose bright tops for summer or warmer tones for fall.

"Earth tones"—shades of brown, beige, tan, rust, maroon, and natural-looking greens like olive and sage—coordinate well with one another and should be accessorized with brown shoes, belts, and purses. Avoid pairing earth tones with vivid primary colors like taxicab yellow, fire-engine red, or swimming-pool blue.

Black shoes, belts, and purses go with dark colors like black, navy, and gray. They also go with intense colors such as red, yellow, kelly green, and

cobalt blue, and pastel tints like pink, aqua, mint green, coral, and baby blue.

Color can be the key to smart accessorizing, too, and it can help fool the eye by drawing attention away from certain figure areas. Think about a vividly colored polka-dot scarf: It can do wonders for the complexion and focus attention on your face—which just might be a great technique to make your presentation more effective. Or consider a Clearly Casual outfit built around khakis; wouldn't a pair of bright driving mocs make that outfit a lot more exciting?

But beware of mixing and matching too many bright accent colors. One or two is fine; more than that and you may risk reminding your coworkers of Mimi in *The Drew Carey Show*.

A SALUTE TO
NAVY BLUE

Fashion legend Diana Vreeland once declared "pink is the navy blue of India." Her wonderful quote instantly conjures up images of a faraway land where bright colors are essential to happiness and fashion. But buried within Madame Vreeland's statement is a tribute to navy blue. Though it may not glow in the moonlight or flatter our complexions as well as pink does, navy blue serves us well, season after season, year after year. It's neutral, it's sophisticated, it's practical, and it's a great alternative to black.

❖ In the **springtime,** navy blue means silk knit cardigans and breezy skirts with white polka dots. ❖ **Summer** brings wide-legged linen pants with drawstring waists—navy, of course—and striped tops with capped sleeves—navy, of course. ❖ **Fall** is a brand-new navy blue suit in chalk-striped wool that will carry you through many autumns to come. ❖ In **winter,** navy blue is your pea coat, your turtleneck sweater, your ankle-length jumper, your silk long underwear, your corduroy pants, your mittens, and the cover of your passport.

TRENDS

Staying in fashion is important for every professional woman. Back in the early 1950s, one style watcher noted, "Wearing the latest modes shows you to be a well-adjusted woman and also a wide-awake one who is in touch with a changing world." Good advice in any era.

TRENDS TO AVOID

Beware of following trends in casual wear rather than trends in business wear. Check the "Top 10 Casual Mistakes for Women," on page 13, for a quick summary of such wardrobe missteps. And remember, provocative clothing is always inappropriate in the office, whether suggestive outfits are currently popular or not. In addition, it's wise to avoid visible tattoos; extremely long fingernails, especially if they're decorated with any kind of "nail art"; bejeweled pieces (rhinestone-studded belt buckles, jackets, jeans pockets, etc.); extreme jewelry (shoulder-sweeping earrings; multiple earrings, bracelets, necklaces, or rings; upper-arm bracelets; toe rings; etc.); and all visible piercings (except for one, or maybe two, tiny holes in each earlobe).

There is a difference between "fashionable" and "trendy," however. Many trendy pieces have such short shelf lives that they're impractical investments for working women. Worse, a number of trends are too silly, sexy, or flashy ever to wear in the office. If you're serious about your career, why wear Lucite-heeled platform shoes or corset-boned tops? You can do better.

The best strategy for fashion-conscious women is to stick with tried-and-true wardrobe basics, then accent them with fun accessories. Depending on your level of casual and your desire to follow the latest trends, you might try them in small doses: dressy boots in an interesting color, a hot new purse by a top designer, a chain belt on low-riding trousers, exceptionally stylish eyeglasses, a great scarf worn as a headband, a wide leather belt with a decorative buckle, a faux fur piece at the collar of a jacket or sweater, or a piece of interesting jewelry.

Remember the tips about accessorizing with color. You can also use color to freshen up a look and stay on top of the trends. Every season certain colors or shades seem to pop up everywhere. One spring it might be a pale orange or a swimming-pool blue, while winter brings rich greens or a warm burgundy. Choose a new top, an accent piece, or a few accessories in currently popular colors and pair them with classic pants and skirts to keep your look up-to-date.

SCARF
Paisley chiffon scarf,
camel/blue

SWEATER
Fine-gauge cotton jewel-neck
sweater, cream

SEPARATES
Silk jacket and pleated
pants, charcoal heather

SHOES
Low strap pumps, red

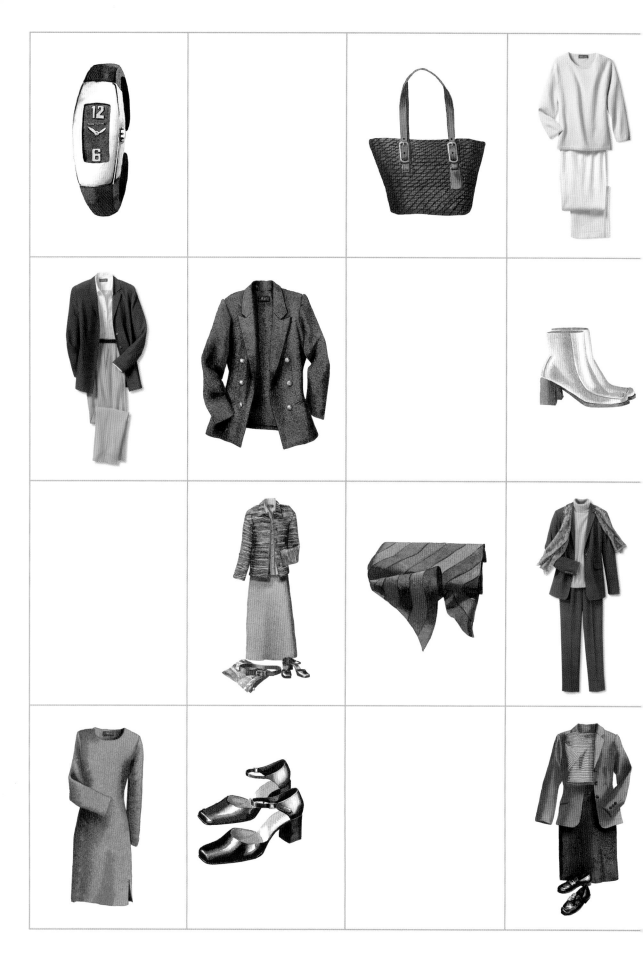

3
THE ELEMENTS OF STYLE

THREE

"The basic wardrobe is the core of

any fashion scheme, and it is hard to be consistently well dressed unless some all-over plan built around such a core is used. The items in the basic wardrobe . . . are the really good things you buy to wear for a long time and to combine with other things that may be more frivolous and of the moment."

These words of wisdom appeared in 1951 in *Family Circle's Complete Book of Beauty and Charm*. And yet their message is as true today as it was the day it was written—right around the time that *I Love Lucy* premiered on prime-time television and China, Israel, and India allowed women to vote.

History lessons aside, there is a certain essential skill that comes into play when building a business wardrobe. Smart women start with classic pieces that comprise the building blocks of good outfits. For maximum effect and efficiency, these basic elements should be: (1) of the highest quality you can afford; (2) wearable for at least three seasons of each year; (3) compatible with all sorts of other pieces in your present and future closet; and (4) timeless in style.

Of course, your building-block pieces should also fit you beautifully (hire a tailor, if needed), and make you feel invincible when you put them on.

ALL ABOUT
JACKETS

In business, it helps to know who your friends are. And just in case you weren't sure, the jacket (aka blazer) is one of your best friends. Why? Because it can make you look sharp, sophisticated, and in control, even if you just threw it on over jeans and a T-shirt ten seconds ago.

For much of European and American history, tailored jackets were worn exclusively by men, as part of a uniform—military, professional, political, or sporting. Coco Chanel is generally credited with breaking that gender barrier. As early as 1906, she was adapting traditional men's riding jackets to suit her own needs, and shortly thereafter she introduced her designs to a fashionable female public.

Chanel believed in practical garments that could be put on and taken off at will—without the assistance of a lady's maid who was forced to struggle with endless rows of hooks, tiny buttons, and complicated undergarments.

Comfort and practicality were radical concepts in early-twentieth-century women's wear. Equally outrageous was Chanel's insistence that the pockets on the jackets she designed be usable. In 1958, *Vogue* lauded Chanel suits for having "real pockets, made to hold a key, a lighter, whatever. . . ."

Besides being flattering to most women's bodies, jackets have always looked professional and have offered endless versatility. You can pair a blazer with a tailored blouse or shirt for a take-charge executive style, or layer the same piece over a knit top or turtleneck for casual charm.

JACKETS TO AVOID

- Fur-collared jackets or blazers
- Denim jackets
- Zippered fleece or nylon cover-ups
- Windbreaker-style jackets
- Jackets with slogans or prominent logos
- Any jacket intended for sports

REMEMBER THE MAINTENANCE

Jackets and blazers need to be dry-cleaned, as do most dress pants, dresses, and some sweaters. Keep this in mind when shopping, especially when you're tempted by light-colored items. Dry-cleaning is expensive and may shorten the life of fine garments. Some experts say that clothing should be dry-cleaned no more than twice a year. Between wearings, air out your jackets and blazers, spot-clean as needed, and refresh the fabric with a good brushing.

Plenty of confusion surrounds women's jacket/blazer options, however. Even in Chanel's time, the terms "jacket" and "blazer" were almost interchangeable when applied to women's wear—and they still are today. One exception is the double-breasted, brass-buttoned blazer—usually seen in navy blue—which is a direct descendent of British Royal Navy uniforms originally worn by the crew of the H.M.S. *Blazer*. Americans invented a single-breasted version, and thus the name still clings to tailored jackets that feature open collars with flat-lying, notched lapels, multiple buttons at the cuffs, and flap pockets at each hip.

Structured jackets (including the classic blazer) are considered dressier than unstructured jackets. Not sure which is which? If the jacket in question is lined, follows the contours of the body via a series of darts, has padded or reinforced shoulders, and has extra interfacing in the collar, lapels, and placket area, it definitely qualifies as structured.

Jackets are usually considered unstructured if they're made of flowing fabrics, especially knits; if they hang loosely in the shoulder area; and if they lack a lining, a nipped waistline, or some sort of closure. In general, zippered jackets are more casual than jackets with buttons.

Single-breasted jackets can be worn buttoned or unbuttoned, as the mood strikes. Double-breasted jackets, however, should always remain buttoned up.

Jacket sleeves should end just below the wrist bone. The shoulder seams on a well-fitting jacket should echo your natural shoulder line. Oversized shoulders can make you look as if you're wearing a man's blazer; too-small shoulders might make you look as if you bought the jacket in the children's department or as if you're bursting out at the seams.

A BLAZER/JACKET SAMPLER
(Ranging loosely from dressiest to most casual)

THREE-BUTTON JACKET, CHARCOAL GRAY

CLASSIC DOUBLE-BREASTED BLAZER, NAVY

BOUCLÉ BLAZER, TOBACCO/MULTI

BUTTONLESS MOHAIR BLAZER, CAMEL

RAYON/LINEN BLAZER, SOFT PINK

PLACKET-FRONT BLAZER, PERIWINKLE

DENIM BLAZER

CORDUROY BIG SHIRT, SAGE

1
B L A Z E R →

Stretch Twill Blazer
Three-Button, Soft Black

A classic black blazer, in a durable, multi-season fabric, can carry you through countless tricky situations, from unpredictable business trips to unexpected news conferences. As long as it's well made and fits you in the sleeve, shoulders, bust, waist, and hips, this ever-ready staple will dress up or down at a moment's notice and always make you look good.

It's not just a building block; it's a cornerstone of the business casual wardrobe.

ALMOST A SUIT

BUTTONED BLAZER
paired with

✳ Microfiber broadcloth shirt, pale rose
✳ Silk scarf, multicolor, tied ascot-style under spread collar (top two or three buttons open)

3
W A Y S

BEST OF BOTH WORLDS

BUTTONED BLAZER
paired with

* Mock turtleneck, true blue
* Large, freeform spiral-shaped, matte silver brooch, pinned to blazer at upper right between collar and shoulder

CLEARLY CASUAL

BUTTONED BLAZER
paired with

* Split-cap-sleeve tee, red-and-white striped
* Big silver hoop earrings (thin)

BUSINESS BASICS
A MINI-WORKBOOK FOR YOUR WARDROBE

Creating a work wardrobe without breaking the bank can seem like a daunting task. But don't despair! By keeping a couple of simple ideas in mind, you can use what you already own and acquire a few key basics to build around. You'll wind up with a wardrobe that works for you while you're at work—without sucking up your entire paycheck in the process. With a little forethought and discernment, you'll never again stand in front of the mirror and say, "I have nothing to wear!" or even, "Does this go together?" (Well, if not "never" maybe "very seldom"!)

GO FOR WHAT'S VERSATILE

No blouse is an island. Same goes for blazers, pants, dresses, skirts, and sweaters. Every piece you add to your closet should coordinate with a number of items you already own, in order to create a variety of outfits. Before shopping, you may want to devise a baseline palette for your work wardrobe, so that the clothing you purchase fits into a general color scheme.

NOT TOO HOT, NOT TOO COLD

The season of a piece should be versatile, as well. Avoid buying anything that's strictly for very cold or very warm weather. Instead, choose multiseason pieces that can be layered as needed. Just as men can select suits in heavier wool or "three-season" fabrics, you can choose to buy the more expensive building blocks—blazers, trousers, and the like—in fabrics and weights that will work nearly year-round. Tropical wool and gabardine are two good choices. Pieces in new microfiber formulations are excellent as well, especially if you travel for business, because they shed water and wrinkles beautifully.

QUALITY EQUALS VALUE

Even if you're just starting out in business, you should buy the best-quality garments you can afford. Not only do well-made clothes look and fit better, but they also last a long time. And they can be taken in or let out, should your weight shift from season to season.

BE TIMELESS

When choosing basics for your wardrobe, pretend you're from Paris. There, women are famous for investing in classic pieces. It's no wonder that the recipe for Parisian chic is equal parts beauty and brains. Be French: Buy with the future in mind.

CARE AND MAINTENANCE

Dry-cleaning costs are part and parcel of having a wardrobe full of structured garments such as blazers, coats, tailored trousers, many dresses, and certain skirts. Even unstructured clothes, such as sweaters and blouses, may insist upon a semiannual trip to the dry cleaners. If you're a Traditional Tailored gal, you'd better get used to the high cost of wardrobe maintenance. If your dress code is more casual, however, you can save oodles of dough by choosing garments that are machine- or hand-washable.

WHAT YOU NEED

Generally speaking, a basic business casual wardrobe includes

Three or more blazers, jackets, or cardigans

Three to five shirts or blouses

Four to six knit tops (including T-shirts and polo shirts)

Three or more sweaters of various weights and styles, including cardigans or twinsets and turtlenecks

At least two skirts

One or two simple dresses

Two or more pairs of tailored trousers in year-round fabrics

Three or more pairs of casual pants, such as chinos or microfiber slacks

Three to five pairs of leather shoes (pumps, boots, loafers, and/or flats)

ALL ABOUT
PANTS

If you were born in 1957, you might remember that crazy afternoon in sixth grade when it was announced over the P.A. system that all female students were, from that day forward, allowed to wear pants to school.

It had been a long time coming. Katharine Hepburn had worn them proudly thirty years earlier, but it had taken a homegrown army of "women's libbers" to give grade-school girls the gift of warm, practical, comfortable trousers in 1968.

Sadly, in the business world, it's been within only the last few decades that trousers have become entirely acceptable for high-profile professional women at work.

Gladly, the rules of business casual put function before fallacy. Thus, there are myriad styles of women's pants, ranging from exquisite slacks to faded jeans, that may be right for enlightened workplaces.

To understand who's who in the world of two-legged garments, it helps to know that virtually every pair of trousers fits into one of two basic categories: "tailored" or "casual."

Tailored trousers are usually made of fine fabrics that drape well, such as wool, wool blends, or linen. Most styles feature constructed waistbands that are designed to encircle a woman's natural waistline, are lined all the way down to the ankles, have pockets that lie flat against the body, and can be altered to achieve a perfect fit. Zippers are usually in the front or back.

Casual pants are associated with easy-care fabrics such as twill, corduroy, denim, and microfiber mixes. Their waistbands—inside and out—are made from the same material as the pants and often rest below a woman's natural waistline. Casual styles include chinos, jeans, fly-front, yoke-waist, side-zip, and virtually any pant that isn't lined. Happily, many casual pants can be thrown in the washing machine (unlike tailored trousers, which usually require dry-cleaning).

Pants are boring only until you learn their secrets. By now, you've deduced that tailored trousers are favored in Traditional Tailored, Almost a Suit, and Best of Both Worlds situations. You've also figured out that lovely, expensive trousers can be custom-fitted to drape perfectly on your body. As for casual pants, which work for Best of Both Worlds and Clearly Casual settings . . . well, if you find the right size and brand, you can buy them in bulk and always have a fresh pair right out of the dryer.

Here are trouser/pant details you need to know: Cuffs are appropriate for most tailored pants as well as for certain casual styles, notably chinos. Whether or not you opt for cuffs, the general rule for tailored trousers is that the legs should be long enough that your ankles aren't visible while standing or walking. Slim, tapered pants (sometimes called "cigarette" pants) can be shorter—just below or a few inches above the ankle bone. Certain wide-legged trousers and flared pants are designed to be worn with higher-heeled boots or shoes; as such, they look best in a longer length that ends just below the top of the heel. Some wide-legged pants are meant to end just below the calf—the best office-friendly ones are made of dressier fabrics, like linen. Elastic waistbands can be a fashion statement, if they're sleek and wide and lie flat against the torso. However, if you choose elasticized waistbands for comfort or fit, be sure that the puckered areas are concealed by a belt, a jacket, or an untucked top.

At one time, plain-front trousers were considered more casual than pleated styles. That's no longer the case. In fact, plain-front pants can lend a contemporary look to dressed-up ensembles.

QUINTESSENTIAL PANTS

ALMOST A SUIT

Tropical-weight-wool trousers, light charcoal heather

Rayon/linen trousers, dark navy

Classic flat-front pants, black

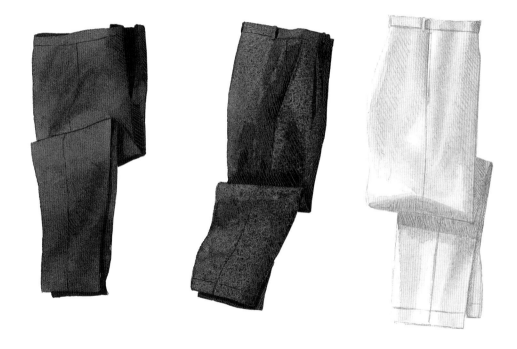

Stretch flannel pants, chocolate

Tailored twill pants, pleated, true navy

Contour chinos, cuffed, dusty tan

QUINTESSENTIAL PANTS

CLEARLY CASUAL

  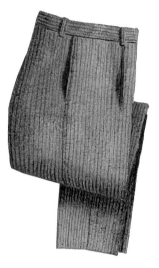

Flat-front knit pants, wide leg, black

Flat-front stretch pants, black

Corduroy pants, dark sage

LET'S TALK ABOUT JEANS

Americans love jeans. We live in the land of dungarees; those tough, honest trousers represent our rugged individualism, our collective pioneering spirit. We all wear 'em. Grandmas and babies. Cowboys and accountants. Rappers, figure skaters, new immigrants, old Yankees. The question is: Should we wear them to the office?

According to one wide-reaching survey, a whopping 86 percent of Americans believe that "neat" jeans are appropriate for designated casual days. Yet a number of tricky issues cling to the jeans question. The biggest problem is that they're available in such a wide range of styles and not all of these styles are office-friendly. Besides the traditional boot-cut or straight-leg models with rivets and topstitching, there are oversized hip-hop jeans that droop below the hip line; trendy bell-bottoms studded with gems; faded jeans with torn knees; stone-washed jeans with pleats and cuffs from another era; and jeans emblazoned with prominent designer logos—to name only a few.

If you choose to include jeans in your professional wardrobe, keep these pointers in mind. ❖ Look for jeans-style pants in stretch twill. They'll keep their shape (and flatter yours) much longer than denim. ❖ Solid-color jeans in any shade but indigo blue are good choices for the office, because they read more like casual pants than jeans. Just make sure to retire them when they become faded or saggy. ❖ If you're going for blue jeans, steer clear of pale or washed-out shades in the office. The darker the better. ❖ Only wear jeans that fit you well and flatter your figure. It isn't easy for women to find their dream jeans, but it's worth the extra shopping time. ❖ Classic five-pocket jeans are always, well, classic. If you stray from the style, go dressier—not more casual. A great pair of slim-leg flares might work, for example, but carpenter jeans or cargo pants could send you into the "dangerously casual" zone. ❖ Update your jeans wardrobe regularly. Favorite dungarees may get softer and more comfy with time, but they're often kept in circulation way past their expiration dates.

ALL ABOUT
SKIRTS

One of the great things about business casual policies is that they liberate women from the tyranny of the skirt.

If you believe that, then you need to rethink your skirt options. What is easier to wear than a long skirt in a fluid knit, paired with flats or boots? What outfit is as crisp and simple as a knee-length skirt and a plain shirt or sweater? What piece can increase the versatility of your wardrobe faster than a little black skirt? No casual closet would be complete without a few good skirts.

As with trousers, the most refined skirts are tailored. That is, they're made of enduring fabrics like wool, silk, and fine blends; have reinforced waists and invisible zippers; and are fully lined.

Less dressy are semistructured and unstructured skirts. These might be airy, tulip-hemmed numbers in bright polyester prints; slim, stretchy columns of jersey; long expanses of comfy cotton knits . . . the list is almost endless.

Details do much to determine the casual quotient of a skirt, and it's wise to pay attention to them. Skirts with belt loops, darts for fit, a tab waist, and a small rear vent are built like fine tailored trousers and work exceedingly well in the Traditional Tailored and Almost a Suit categories. Skirts with stretchy elastic waistbands, no darts, and more flowing silhouettes can be considered more casual, regardless of their length, and fit the Best of Both Worlds and Clearly Casual categories quite neatly. In any category, a skirt almost always seems just a little dressier than pants.

However, beware of "skorts" (combinations of skirts and shorts) or any type of golf skirt, as they are meant for sports and the outdoors and have no place in the office, no matter how hot the weather may be.

Kilts and other plaid pleated skirts can be quite conservative. In the business environment, remember that they should never be worn with socks, knee-length or otherwise. Keep in mind as well that patchwork patterns and lots of colorful embroidery can also make a skirt more fit for casual wear than for the conference room.

The most casual skirts look suspiciously like pants but have a whole different cachet. A denim skirt, for example—ankle-length, above the knee, or somewhere in between— might have the lived-in feel of your favorite pair of jeans but earns major dress-up points simply because it's a skirt. The same magic trick is performed even more effectively by corduroy, chino, and twill skirts.

Standard skirt lengths are 21 inches, 24 inches, 26 inches, and 34 inches. In traditional businesses, you can't go wrong with a knee-length skirt (which, depending on your height, is 21 to 24 inches). Longer is okay, too. In more casual environments, hems fluctuate. If you're a Best of Both Worlds or Clearly Casual gal—and you've got the figure for it—you can probably top out at above the knee (about 16 inches), as long as the skirt is fairly conservative and is worn with stockings or tights. Shorter than that deserves real thought and should be saved for creative Clearly Casual environments.

QUINTESSENTIAL SKIRTS

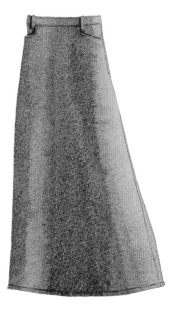

Wool skirt, knee-length, black

Skirt, mid-calf length, plum

Wool flannel "riding" skirt, long, olive

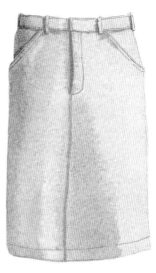

Wrap skirt, slightly below the knee, camel

Cotton knit full skirt, true navy

Chino skirt, knee-length, field khaki

ALL ABOUT
SHIRTS

"Top": a simple little word with a big, complicated job. This multifaceted category of clothing includes shirts, blouses, knits, turtlenecks, polos, tees, and more—a striped rugby shirt; a delicate silk blouse. Which tops are for you? Read on.

Women's shirts are the direct offspring of men's shirts, and they share many of the same features, including collars, plackets, sleeves, and buttons. Yet the range of women's styles is greater by far. Women can choose from tailored oxford shirts with button-down collars, stretchy shirts with wide collars and elbow-length sleeves, and silk confections with scoop necks and poetic cuffs that can only be called "blouses."

What, you may ask, is the difference between a "blouse" and a "shirt"? It's a fine line. Blouses tend to be softer in shape, made from more delicate materials, and might feature gossamer fabric, embroidery, dramatic sleeves, fluttering cuffs, or jeweled buttons. Perhaps the best definition is this: Any shirt that's too feminine for a man to wear can safely be called a blouse. Remember Jerry Seinfeld's infamous "puffy shirt"? Yup; a blouse.

When determining the casual quotient of a shirt or blouse, there are many factors to consider, and each is relative to another.

FABRICS (from most dressy to most casual): silk, rayon, faille, linen, cotton-poly blends, end-on-end or poplin cotton, oxford cloth, seersucker, flannel, corduroy, denim. *Note:* The dressiest fabrics are the smoothest or

SHIRTS TO AVOID

- Shirts that are too tight or too short (no abdomens on view at the office)
- Translucent or see-through shirts and sheer lace tops
- T-shirt tops with unfinished or ragged edges
- Microfleece tops
- Shirts with printed logos or slogans
- Completely sequined or beaded tops
- Spaghetti-strap tops worn without a cardigan or jacket
- Any lingerie-like camisole top
- Leather shirts with dangling feathers or beads
- Shirts with corset-style lacing
- Sweatshirts

shiniest. The finer the weave, the more formal the fabric. Shiny fabrics have an evening feel and should be avoided in the office, especially in business casual environments.

SLEEVES (from most dressy to most casual): long sleeved, three-quarter length, elbow length, short sleeved, cap sleeved, sleeveless.

COLLARS (from most dressy to most casual): straight collar, collarless, scoop collar, notched collar, button-down collar, Peter-Pan collar, and styles that are meant to be buttoned at the neck.

PLACKETS: In case you've forgotten, the placket is the vertical strip along which your shirt opens and closes. It usually extends from the center of your collar to the bottom of your shirt hem and features buttons and buttonholes. Common placket styles, in order from most dressy to most casual, are: covered by an extension of fabric, so that the buttons are hidden; folded back, so that the buttons show but there is no obvious seam along the edge of the fabric; and "set on," in which the placket is emphasized (and reinforced) by two seams that bracket the buttons, top to bottom.

COLORS (from most dressy to most casual): white, off-white, China blue, medium blue, pale colors and pastels, strong colors.

PATTERNS (from most dressy to most casual): conservative stripes, fine stripes and checks, subtle florals and prints, bold stripes or checks, high-contrast florals and prints.

CUFFS: Long-sleeved shirts can have two basic types of cuffs: French cuffs (which take cuff links or similar fasteners) or buttoned cuffs. Unlike men's shirts, women's shirts with French cuffed sleeves are not inherently more formal than those with buttoned cuffs. Women also don't wear cuff links as a rule. Rather, women's French cuffed shirts are often fastened with simple fabric or silk-cord knots that function like cuff links.

QUINTESSENTIAL SHIRTS

ALMOST A SUIT

BEST OF BOTH WORLDS

Classic broadcloth shirt with turn-
back cuffs, pink

Oxford button-down, pink

CLEARLY CASUAL

When shopping for a shirt or blouse, make sure it has a button positioned directly between your breasts. Sounds strange? Take the advice to heart—proper button placement is what will keep your blouse from straining or gaping at the bust. Same goes for cardigans and wrap shirts. Create an imaginary X at the significant intersection and don't buy anything unless you have the proper closure.

Long-sleeved T-shirt, pink

ALL ABOUT
SWEATERS

The original "sweater" was a heavy blanket worn by horses. It was designed to make the animals perspire during workouts—thus, the name. These equestrian blankets provided the inspiration for the striped knitted sweaters worn by French sailors. In the 1920s, gentlemen of means began sporting their own versions of the French seamen's style. Ten years later, the sweater made its way into the realm of women's wear with the help of two designers: Madeleine Vionnet, who popularized stretchy clothing, and Coco Chanel, who introduced the twinset. (In Great Britain, sweaters are known as jumpers, by the way.)

Today, the sweater is so versatile, it's practically acrobatic: wispy little shells to be worn under jackets or overshirts, chunky cotton turtlenecks, snug cable-knit crews, colorful cardigans that turn mere pants and tops into outfits, sweater jackets that stand in for blazers, and so much more. Every woman can benefit from a great collection of sweaters in her working wardrobe.

The finer the gauge, the more dressy a sweater becomes. The thicker and chunkier the knit, the more casual the sweater is considered. Big, thick, wide-ribbed cotton knits send a very different message from finely tailored two-ply cashmere tops.

The woman who invests in a few matching or coordinating fine-gauge sweater sets will have a substantial start on her business casual wardrobe. Fine-gauge cotton, linen, silk, or cashmere sweaters can form a solid, seasonless foundation for your workday closet.

The image of a sweater set need not be restricted to the classic twinset of a jewel-neck short-sleeved top with a matching long-sleeved crewneck cardigan. Think about combinations of collared, jewel-neck, or

V-necked cardigans and sleeveless shells, turtlenecks, or mocknecks. The same jewel-neck short-sleeved sweater can work like a chameleon, appearing under a blazer with a dressy scarf, pairing with a matching collared V-necked cardigan, or topping off a pair of chinos on its own, moving through Almost a Suit to Clearly Casual workplaces with the greatest of ease.

Sweaters are so versatile that their variations can seem endless, but they do share some details of construction. They are all knit from some type of yarn, whether it be Mongolian cashmere, stretchy polyester, or cotton and linen. Yarns are made of fibers, and natural fibers such as cotton may be combed before spinning, increasing the softness of the yarn. The yarn itself can have a number of strands, or plys, twisted around one another, increasing its thickness. Yarn dyeing (rather than dyeing the finished sweater) makes for richer, long-lasting color. The edges of the sweater can be neatly hemmed or rib-knit into a variety of patterns; rib-knit hems and sleeves are quite durable, keeping their shape well, wearing after wearing. Turtlenecks may have seams in the neck or be knit as a seamless column or tube. The best-fitting sweaters are often those in which the panels are knit to size and then sewn or linked together.

SWEATERS TO AVOID

- Sweaters with low-cut necklines revealing pronounced cleavage
- Sweaters that reveal undergarments (bras, bra straps, sports bras, corsets)
- Halter-style sweaters
- Tube-style sweaters
- Polartec or thick microfleece sweaters
- Sweaters that are too tight
- Sweaters with sweatshirt details such as hoods or pouch pockets

In the world of business casual, the way a sweater fits can raise or lower its casual quotient. Generally, the longer the sweater, the slouchier the shoulders, and the more relaxed the neck, the more casual the sweater appears. Seams that fall neatly on one's natural shoulders, sleeves that reach the wrists, and a length that falls at or just slightly below the waist mark a dressier style. Remember the importance of thickness and layering, too—a bulky sweater will not look right under a blazer and may stretch the shoulders or prevent the buttons from closing in front, neither of which are desirable in any workplace setting.

QUINTESSENTIAL SWEATERS

ALMOST A SUIT

BEST OF BOTH WORLDS

Merino wool twinset, camel

Sweater with a tie neck, wine

Cotton cowl-neck sweater, yellow

Cable cardigan, navy

Fisherman sweater, ivory

Chunky turtleneck, striped

ALL ABOUT
DRESSES

The best thing about a dress is that you can step into it, put on earrings (perhaps), stockings (maybe), shoes or boots (definitely), and voilà—you're out the door. So easy. So efficient.

It's a shame that some women consider dresses too fussy and femmy for business casual wear. Is the name to blame? Maybe. "Dress" is the root word of "dressy," after all. Some of us might have unpleasant memories of stiff Sunday-school frocks with itchy crinolines or toxic bridesmaids' gowns studded with bows.

In the real world, lots of contemporary dresses are perfectly appropriate for all sorts of casual and semicasual situations. What's more, many are blissfully comfortable.

Some dresses act like suits and fit into the Traditional Tailored or Almost a Suit categories. Think of the coatdress, which is essentially a knee-length blazer or trench, often distinguished by deep lapels that beg for a pearl-encrusted brooch; and the jacket dress, a two-piece garment featuring a simple sheath topped by a coordinating jacket or lightweight coat.

As dresses become more relaxed, they lose their darts, pleats, and linings. The fluid wrap dress, pioneered by Diane von Furstenberg, is an enduring style that manages to be ladylike even while it emphasizes feminine curves. In the same family are silk, rayon, and microfiber dresses that might be long or short, fitted or full, patterned or plain, with Empire waists, tulip hems, poet sleeves, scooped necklines . . . the available variety is astounding. As long as they're not too flirty, these dresses can rule Best of Both workplaces.

Most casual—and cozy—are loose-fitting dresses made of cotton knits or other soft fabrics. Anybody who thinks that dresses are uncomfortable has never stepped out in cascading A-lines that barely skim the body. These Clearly Casual/Best of Both Worlds garments are basically overgrown T-shirts or sweaters that have taken a good thing and extended it to the knees, the calves, or the ankles.

Dresses are easy to own, easy to wear. But they're not foolproof. The two most common mistakes in the dress department are wearing dresses that are too fancy and wearing dresses that look dowdy.

The Too-Fancy Zone is occupied by dresses that are shiny, sparkly, velvety, gauzy, poufy, lacy, or deliberately sexy. Curvy cocktail dresses and silvery sheaths are obvious no-nos, but even a plain dress with satin piping or a bit of sequined embroidery can cross the line. Remember this: If you'd wear it to a wedding, a nightclub, your thirtieth birthday party, a high-school reunion, or the Kentucky Derby, don't wear it to work.

Dowdiness happens when women wear dresses long beyond their expiration dates. These dresses are often cotton, blousy, and long, virtual caftans that provide camouflage. If that woman is you, get out there and buy at least three stylish new dresses that feel great, flatter the body, and still provide a gentle disguise on days when you need to hide.

DON'T LET THIS HAPPEN TO YOU

In May 2001, the Colorado Supreme Court issued a dress code governing the appearance of attorneys in courtrooms throughout the state. Male and female lawyers were ordered to wear white shirts, red-and-white striped ties, and blue blazers with the Colorado state seal on the pocket. This "court uniform" allows men to wear tan slacks in the summer months and gray flannel trousers in winter. Women must wear plaid skirts year-round and white ankle socks. The drastic move was made in response to a general abuse of casual dress codes, which had resulted in lawyers' showing up to argue cases in hiking boots, black jeans, jackets bearing "Gnarly Dude" logos, and the like. The new uniform was based on the recommendations of fashion consultants and parochial school principals. Ladies and gentlemen: Don't let confusion and abuse of "casual" jeopardize your personal freedom of style.

QUINTESSENTIAL DRESSES

ALMOST A SUIT

Jacket dress, chocolate tweed

Wool dress, sapphire

Ribbed knit turtleneck dress, teal

Simple cotton knit dress,
true navy

OUTERWEAR

How do you dress when you're coming and going? Don't be casual with your choice of outerwear; often it's your overcoat, jacket, trench, or slicker that creates both a first and a last impression. Considering that most women wear only one or two primary pieces of outerwear per season, it's essential that those cover-ups send the right message.

If you live in a wintry climate, invest in a good wool coat. It will keep you warm and stylish in all kinds of situations.

The level of a woman's casual style can be measured by the length of her coat. If it falls between the ankle and the knee, it can be worn anywhere. Above the knee to fingertip length can work for Best of Both Worlds and Clearly Casual outfits; any shorter and it qualifies as a jacket. Go ahead and use a jacket as a topper for trousers or skirts, but be aware that it lends a casual look when worn as outerwear.

In very relaxed workplaces, the parka is the winter wear of choice. Parkas look fine when they're layered over casual trousers and tops, but they should not be worn over dresses, skirts, blazers, or proper pantsuits.

Zippers are more laid-back than buttons, which means that a pea coat fits into more situations than a windbreaker, even if the two jackets are made of the same fabric.

Foul-weather gear should be reserved for foul weather. The only exception is the classic trench coat, which is seasonally neutral and can be worn in rain, sleet, snow, fog, and sunshine.

When it's cold outside, even the most sophisticated women run the risk of looking like third-graders dressed for a snowball fight. Be aware of the levels of business casual attached to your outdoor accessories.

GLOVES/MITTENS: The most businesslike are sleek, supple gloves in black or brown leather (to coordinate with your winter coat). For extra warmth, find a pair with a thin lining of wool or cashmere. Knit gloves, or those made of fabric, are somewhat more casual; nylon or microfiber gloves with bulky linings are reminiscent of ski gloves and should be worn only with parkas or down coats. As for mittens . . . they are ultra-casual, and not particularly practical (ever try fumbling for keys in a pair of mitts?).

Style note: *Avoid fingerless gloves.*

SCARVES/MUFFLERS: If you want to make an elegant statement while keeping chills at bay, tuck a patterned silk scarf, ascot-style, inside the collar of your wool coat or trench. Pashmina, cashmere, and fine-gauge wool scarves also give a polished look if they're worn under—not over—a coat. More relaxed are knitted scarves and microfiber mufflers; these gain a Clearly Casual rating when allowed to dangle outside of a coat or jacket, especially if the scarf is extra-long and trimmed in fringe.

HATS: If you're dressing to impress, take care to coordinate your hat with your coat. A close-fitting, furry hat might be fine for winter weather; a brimmed, blocked hat could be fetching in fall and spring; and a cute rain hat could serve you well on wet days. In every case, the hat should complement the style and color of the coat. Berets can be a godsend for women in every category, because they're available in a huge range of colors and work well in fall, winter, and spring. If your workplace is casual enough that you can wear pea coats and parkas, remember that bright or oddly shaped ski hats are better left to teenage snowboarders. Instead, stick with simple styles and reasonable colors. Ear-warming headbands and fuzzy earmuffs are also acceptable for casual dressers and have a special advantage: no "hat hair."

Style note: *Avoid hunting hats with earflaps, unless you want to look like Elmer Fudd. Forget baseball-style caps, too, or any headgear emblazoned with slogans or logos.*

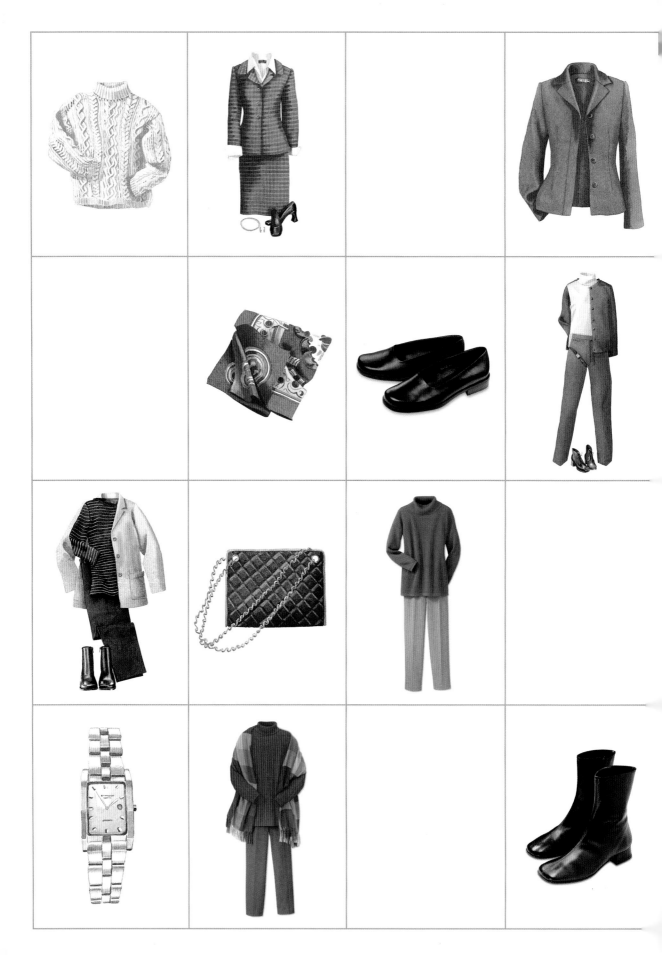

4

ACCESSORIES

FOUR

Business casual is riddled with

restrictions (and for good reason), but there is freedom in the mix, especially with regard to accessories. Shoes, scarves, jewelry, belts, and purses are the most personal items in a working woman's wardrobe, and these decorative elements can turn a generic outfit into a one-of-a-kind fashion statement.

Accessorizing is fun; when done right, it can also be powerful. One study, cited in a 1995 report, showed that women who had a strong individual sense of fashion were generally confident, well-liked, emotionally stable, and had high levels of self-esteem.

If you've invested in classic pieces, you can rely on an ever-changing arsenal of accessories to keep your look fresh. A trendy belt can make a plain skirt and blouse seem brand-new, even if you've been wearing them for years; take a basic knit dress, add cool boots and a splashy necklace, and you've got style to spare, without a hefty price tag.

ALL ABOUT
SHOES

In her book *Dress Code*, Toby Fischer-Mirkin states that shoes "can divulge whether we think of ourselves as daring or distinguished, a conservative or a free spirit. Wearing a particular shoe style is one of the easiest ways to express our emotions. Each style has a soul of its own."

SHOES TO AVOID

- Clear-plastic-heeled shoes
- Shoes or boots with stiletto heels
- Shoes with extremely pointy toes, high platforms, lacing up the leg, wraparound ankle straps, or other provocative details
- Sandals
- Clogs
- Thigh-high boots, work boots, hiking boots
- Athletic shoes of any kind, unless they don't *look* like athletic shoes

And a sole of its own. When it comes to finding appropriate footwear for business casual, it is often practicality, not the urges of fashion, that inform our choices. Women who work in so-called glamour industries might be able to prance around in stilettos and ankle straps (think Samantha Jones in *Sex and the City*), but those of us who aren't whisked around in limousines from one fabulous event to another need shoes that will wear well, feel good, and coordinate with our working wardrobes.

Virtually every woman in business, no matter what her level of business casual, should invest in at least one pair of high-quality, neutral-colored leather pumps (black, brown, and navy are standards of choice). Even if she wears them only a few times a year, women's pumps are similar to men's neckties in that when you need them, you really need them.

Okay, you've got your conservative pumps. Now what? As a woman, it is your right and privilege to fall in love with every mule, slide, slingback, and boot that catches your eye. But you can't have them all—where would you put them? More to the point, where would you wear them? Though footwear fashions change from year to year, only a limited number of styles work well on the business casual floor. And it's your job to find them.

Serious shoe-shopping begins with a willingness to spend more for quality. In spite of what Star Jones may pitch in her commercials, cheap shoes are rarely a bargain. Most are made from synthetic materials, which (1) don't expand, and therefore will never "break in" to accommodate your foot; (2) make your feet perspire—which is miserable in any season; and (3) wear badly and can't be polished successfully. Even when an inexpensive shoe is made of leather, its low price usually indicates inferior stitching and construction. High-quality footwear, made of natural materials and constructed by artisans, may cost more up front but will pay for itself in comfort and longevity. Besides, cheap shoes almost always look cheap.

When it comes to determining the dressiness of a shoe, a host of clues are at our fingertips. A leather-soled shoe is dressier than a wooden-soled shoe, and rubber-soled shoes are the most casual of all—especially if the soles are nubbed, lugged, treaded, or otherwise textured.

Smooth leather uppers are fancier than stamped hides like crocodile or snakeskin, which in turn are more formal than pebblegrain, suede, nubuck, woven leather, fabric, or other nonreflective materials.

Flats are more casual than high heels, of course. But height isn't everything. Wood-stacked heels are less dressy than leather-clad heels, and platforms or wedgies are more casual than traditional stiletto, Cuban, or sculpted heels—whether they make you two, three, or even four inches taller than you really are.

Foot exposure is another important aspect of the shoe equation. No matter what the season, footwear that covers your toes and heels is considered most businesslike (and ladylike, in an old-fashioned way). Every millimeter of exposed skin subtracts formality points. Slingbacks and fancy mules are okay for Almost a Suit looks; mules, loafers, backless loafers, and stylish shoes with discreetly exposed toes could work with Best of Both Worlds ensembles; strappy sandals, thongs, clogs, and open-toed flats dwell in the Clearly Casual realm.

QUINTESSENTIAL SHOES

ALMOST A SUIT

Pumps, black

Croc-embossed pumps, navy

BEST OF BOTH WORLDS

Kiltie loafers, brown

Short boots, natural

CLEARLY CASUAL

Smooth penny loafers, navy

Lace-up boots, black

Two-piece pumps, black

Chunky skimmers, black

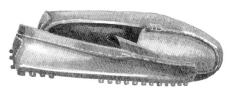

Brazilian driving mocs, dark tan

FOR EACH SHOE, A SEASON

There are some places in this country where a person can get away with wearing white or light-colored shoes year-round. Or not. When in doubt, save your bone pumps and pink slingbacks for that magical period of time between Memorial Day and Labor Day. ❖ It's not okay to commute in sneakers and athletic socks. This trend got its start in the 1980s during the New York City transit strike, when many women in the financial industries had to walk over the Brooklyn Bridge or march for miles down the avenues to reach their Wall Street offices. Most of them wisely gave up their big white sneaks as soon as the strike ended. Few ensembles look less professional than an Almost a Suit outfit ending at the ankles with running shoes. ❖ When contending with rain, snow, ice, and sleet, it's smart to wear all-weather boots or water-repellent shoes, then change into office-appropriate shoes in the ladies' room. Luckily, there are plenty of sturdy, warm, skidproof, and/or weatherproof styles attractive enough to wear on the street.

Boots have their own set of rules. Mid-calf boots with mildly tapered heels (one or two inches high) are considered the most conservative style for women; in business situations, such boots are usually worn under pants or long skirts. The more exotic the boot, the more casual it is considered. Thus, ankle-high boots with kitten heels might fall into the Best of Both Worlds category, while knee-high lace-up boots might be too wild for anything but Clearly Casual outfits. And speaking of Clearly Casual, don't try to get away with work boots, jackboots, or hiking boots in any workplace that isn't relaxed to the max. Even then, keep them safely beneath your pant legs.

Let's not forget the color of your shoes. If you work in a highbrow corporation, your choices are pretty much limited to black, brown, navy, and camel, or maybe bone. Color becomes more acceptable with each level of casual chic. Shiny red slides, pink loafers, sky-blue boots, and two-tone ballerina flats aren't unheard of in Best of Both Worlds and Clearly Casual shoe wardrobes.

Using the above guidelines, we can safely conclude that the most casual shoes are open-toed buckskin slides, in a sage green tone, with thick rubber soles. The most formal shoes are polished black pumps with two-inch heels. In between are brown suede loafers, lavender clogs, stretchy beige ankle boots, metallic sport shoes, and whatever else your imagination—and dress code—will allow.

ALL ABOUT
HOSIERY

As long as women have been dressing up and going to work, hosiery has been an integral part of the professional look. Today, the dressiest stockings are the "ultra-sheer" variety, which are made from extremely fine yarns and have a subtle contouring effect on the leg. On the job, ultra-sheer hose work best when they're matched to one's natural skin tone—or perhaps one shade darker. Black or dark-tinted sheers might be appropriate for certain Traditional Tailored and Almost a Suit ensembles, but more often they're associated with evening wear and can look out of place in the office.

HOSIERY TO AVOID

- Fishnets
- Stockings or tights in vivid colors or pale shades
- Athletic socks
- Stockings attached to garters that have even the vaguest chance of being seen
- Knee-high socks or stockings (except under trousers)

The mid-range of business casual wear is dominated by panty hose made from stretchy, medium-weight yarns. Economical, durable, and disposable, these stockings are the workhorses of a woman's hosiery wardrobe. When it comes to color, "nude" is the optimum shade for day-to-day business, although dark tones (navy, brown, black) can also work, as long as they're matched with shoes of the same color. Don't try to use them to fake a tan—it won't work.

Opaque tights are considered the most casual legwear, especially those that have a high cotton content, thick textured ribbing, or other heavy woven patterns. Tights should always be dark in color (black, brown, or navy). Again, for a polished look, your tights should match your shoes.

Depending on your working situation, you might be able to let your legs be bare. But before you make this choice, be sure that your company dress code allows it and your legs are impeccably shaved or waxed.

Socks should be as dark as or darker than the pants, even if they don't quite match the shoes. Thin socks are dressy. Thick socks are not.

ALL ABOUT
BELTS

Rarely does a woman's belt actually hold up her pants. More often, she wears it to keep her belt loops company or to add style and substance to an outfit.

Generally speaking, thin belts are fancier than wide belts, black belts are dressier than brown belts, and belts with gold-toned buckles are more formal than belts with silver hardware. Beyond these open-to-interpretation guidelines, there is one rule to remember: The color of your belt should match or coordinate with the color of your shoes.

The belts pictured here are fairly standard and conservative. But let's not forget that belts can also function as jewelry for the waist (or hips). On the casual end of the belt rack, you might find wide black belts with silver rivets; modified rodeo belts with big, filigreed buckles; wrap belts that drip fringe; or hip-hugging "slouch" belts with no buckles at all. Just because a belt is unconventional doesn't mean it's banned from Almost a Suit outfits, however. Chain-link belts can make beautiful music on slim skirts, while belts with unusual details (antique coins, gilded borders, turquoise stones) can jazz up an ensemble without putting it over the top.

A BELT SAMPLER
(Ranging loosely from dressiest to most casual)

Croc-embossed belts, dressy, black and brown

Glove leather belts, dressy, navy and brown

Glove leather belts, black, with gold and silvertone buckles

Skinny casual belts, tan and brown

Skinny casual belts, black and red

ALL ABOUT
SCARVES

Question: What can add instant color and artistry to an otherwise generic ensemble? Answer: a scarf.

The scarf is the personal paint box of the working woman. It can be as quiet as a bit of silk peeking out from the pocket of a blazer or as bold as a multicolored square tied around the shoulders of a dress. You can choose vibrant patterns on heavy satin, giddy prints on lengths of sheer chiffon, earthy blocks of color on raw-edged cotton or wool . . . the stroke of color and texture is yours to make, as you choose.

Generally speaking, silk scarves with rolled edges are the highest form of neck decoration. Diaphanous scarves with chiffon aspirations are pretty fancy, too; in cool climates, fine wool, pashmina, and cashmere scarves are upscale favorites. Cotton is more casual; in fact, any nubby or raised texture adds to a scarf's casual quotient, no matter what it's made of. Heavily beaded chiffon, velvet (especially burn-out patterned velvet), thick satin, and lace can paradoxically be too dressy for the office or too funky to wear behind the desk.

Patterns can subtly affect the style of a scarf as well; classic floral, ribbon, paisley, or pictorial patterns with a solid border are somehow a bit more formal than large polka dots or bold stripes. Wide, colorful plaid patterns are most often found on wool scarves, clearly placing them in the outerwear or most casual categories. The familiar white bandanna pattern on navy blue or red cotton squares is another Clearly Casual look, and long fringes can also stretch a scarf closer to the casual end of the spectrum.

What really separates the Almost a Suits from the Clearly Casuals, however, is how a scarf is worn. Tied around the neck and tucked under a blouse or jacket, ascot-style, it gains a subtle elegance that works with even the most formal of businesswear. When a large square is folded into a triangle

A SCARF SAMPLER
(Ranging loosely from dressiest to most casual)

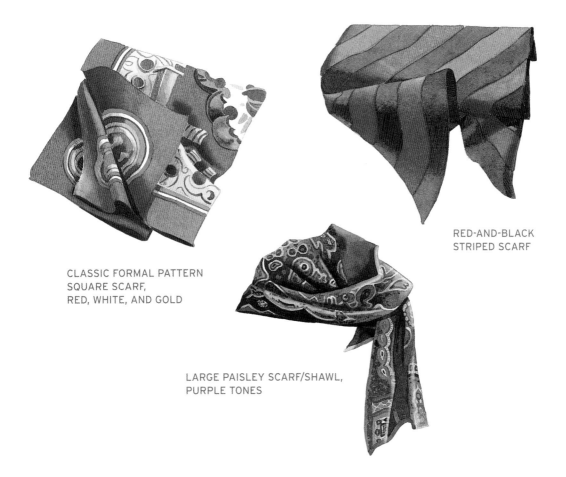

CLASSIC FORMAL PATTERN
SQUARE SCARF,
RED, WHITE, AND GOLD

RED-AND-BLACK
STRIPED SCARF

LARGE PAISLEY SCARF/SHAWL,
PURPLE TONES

and knotted over the shoulders, it's somewhat more casual and falls into the same Almost a Suit or Best of Both Worlds categories as the oblong scarf that's tied at the bust or hangs freely against a jacket, blouse, or dress. Large, woolly scarves can be worn as wraps or shawls, which is most suitable for Best of Both Worlds or Clearly Casual types. Scarves knotted or tied around the head are a bold personal style statement that few choose to make in the office, although a scarf tied as a small headband can be appropriate. Perhaps the most casual look is the neckerchief—a small square tied jauntily around the neck, tips akimbo.

HOW TO TIE A SCARF

HEAD WEAR 1 (HEADBAND)

1. Fold a square on the bias as shown.
2. Wrap around the head and tie in a knot at the base of the hairline in back.

ASCOT STYLE

1. Fold a square scarf into an oblong.
2. Place around the neck and flip one end over the other.

SQUARE KNOT

1. Fold a square scarf into a triangle.
2. Flip one end over the other.
3. Take the upper end around and behind the lower end.
4. Pull through and tighten.
5. Place the knot at the front, side, or back, according to your preference.

HACKING KNOT

1. Fold an oblong scarf in half and drape around the neck.
2. Pull the loose ends through the loop and tighten.

KNOTTED NECK WRAP

1. Fold a square scarf into a triangle.
2. Place the point in front.
3. Cross the ends behind the neck.
4. Tie in front using a square knot.

NECKERCHIEF

1. Fold a square bandanna or scarf on the bias.
2. Wrap around the neck and tie in a knot.
3. Place the knot at the front, side, or back, according to your preference.

HEAD WEAR 2

1. Fold a square scarf into a triangle.
2. Bring down across the forehead and knot in back.

ALL ABOUT
JEWELRY

A glint of gold at the earlobes. A charming circle of silver at the wrist. A stylish watch; a low-key choker; a pretty pendant. Jewelry can add personality and appeal to a business ensemble, but beware: Such accessories must be chosen with great discretion. Nothing can wreck a professional look more thoroughly than the misuse of baubles, bangles, and beads.

As Wendy Wasserstein once noted, "Accessories are the key to fashion. . . . With the right earrings, bracelet, and scarf you will always be very 'too-too.'"

Few women have velvet-lined chests full of Bulgari watches, Mikimoto pearls, and Harry Winston rings. But even a modest collection of interesting pieces (with or without pedigrees) can make you glint and glow in all the right places.

Wear one family of metals at a time. If you're wearing a gold watch, coordinate with gold earrings, a gold-toned belt buckle, et cetera. If you want to don silver hoops, group them with other silver-finish pieces.

Pearls go with pearls. They also go with gold, so long as the gold and pearl pieces are harmonious, style-wise.

Be stingy with gemstones or anything that sparkles. It's fine to wear small diamond studs in your ears (or rubies, sapphires, or amethysts), and of course your wedding band and engagement ring are eternally perfect. But jeweled bracelets, sparkly necklaces, pavé–accented watches, and the like should light up the night, not the day.

Avoid dramatic drop earrings. They tend to overwhelm the face and can look unprofessional in an office environment.

Less is more. The most common jewelry faux pas have nothing to do with the pieces themselves: They have to do with how many pieces are worn at once. To be safe, stick with a maximum of three jewelry accents per outfit. (Count earrings as a single element; don't include rings, unless they are noticeably dramatic; do include watches and decorative belt buckles.) Using this formula, you can be confident wearing combinations such as gold hoops, a chain around your neck, and a gold bangle bracelet; or a silver choker, a silver-toned belt buckle, and a titanium watch; or topaz earrings, a chain belt, and a coordinating cuff bracelet. And so on.

Don't overload your fingers. Rings are wonderfully expressive, but when more than three digits are decorated, the look becomes exaggerated.

Business casual presents a great opportunity to show off your brooches. Nothing can personalize a plain blazer better than a fetching pin at the shoulder. Explore, experiment, enjoy.

Finally, know yourself. If you're large in stature and have a big personality, you're wise to choose bold pieces that match your spirit. If you're an ultramodern minimalist, you might steer away from jewelry altogether. Consider the above pointers, then let your instincts be your guide.

A JEWELRY SAMPLER
(Ranging loosely from dressiest to most casual)

What is more elegant, distinguished, and historic than pearls? (Heck, they're worn by Queen Elizabeth II, Barbara Bush, Joan Rivers, and Wilma Flintstone, to name a few.) A strand of pearls, worn over a blouse or sweater, or peeking out from under a well-made blazer, whispers of high stakes and good breeding. Whether yours are real or beautifully bluffed, wear them—with or without matching earrings—when you want to exude a Traditional Tailored or Almost a Suit aura.

A glint of gold at the throat, wrist, ears, or fingers lends a note of rich authenticity to Almost a Suit or Best of Both Worlds outfits. Remember that less is more when it comes to gold pieces; resist the urge to wear multiple chains around your neck or too many rings on your fingers.

Silver-toned accessories are perfectly matched with Best of Both Worlds and Clearly Casual looks. Here, utility meets beauty in a stainless-steel watch modified from a classic men's design. Pair it with sterling silver earrings, a silver choker, and little more.

This modern, bold-faced watch flaunts an industrial combination of stainless steel and rubber. The cuff-bracelet styling is Clearly Casual and can be complemented with silver hoops in the ears and a choir of platinum, steel, silver, and rubber bangles on the opposite wrist.

DECODING
INVITATIONS

Dressing for work is only part of business casual. In social or business-related events, rules of proper attire evolve on a daily basis. The following primer might help you decode invitations, but whenever you're seriously in doubt about what to wear, phone your host or event organizer in advance. And you're always best off erring on the side of caution—carrying a slightly dressier jacket can let you adjust to the occasion.

Here's what you should wear if the invitation says

WHITE TIE: The most formal of all invitations, this one requires a long evening gown or ball gown, your best jewelry, a clutch bag, and perhaps a pair of evening-length gloves.

BLACK TIE: Your date—lucky him—doesn't have to think twice. All he needs is a black tuxedo. You, on the other hand, must choose between a long gown or a fancy cocktail dress. Dressy suits can also work, but only if they're made from elegant fabrics such as satin, silk, or chiffon.

FORMAL: same as "black tie."

BLACK TIE OPTIONAL: This means you can either follow the rules of black tie or be slightly more casual in a cocktail dress or a dressy suit.

CREATIVE BLACK TIE: Here's your chance to get wild with your dress-up clothes. Think of a cross between the Oscars and the MTV Video Music Awards—if it's a business-related event, however, you're wise to avoid scandalous gowns. Go for something vintage, costumey, sparkly, ultra-glam, or just plain fun.

SEMIFORMAL: festive cocktail dresses or dressy suits.

BUSINESS ATTIRE: When an event is held right after regular working hours, traditional business attire is usually what's expected. If you work in a Best of Both Worlds or a Clearly Casual environment, you may find your-self underdressed for the occasion. When in doubt, wear a dress or an attractive, professional-looking ensemble of the Almost a Suit variety.

ELEGANT CASUAL: stylish and polished, yet also comfortable. Again, go for an Almost a Suit look, perhaps complemented by special jewelry and ultra-chic shoes.

DRESSY CASUAL: Usually means very much the same as "elegant casual." In general, this is a good cue to wear a dress and a pair of heels, perhaps with a string of pearls or special jewelry.

SMART CASUAL: A Best of Both Worlds look will work, but don't wear jeans, very casual pants or shoes, or untailored tops.

CASUAL: The interpretation of this word depends entirely on the event and who is hosting it. If the invitation is to a backyard barbecue, you can be fairly sure that shorts and T-shirts will rule the day. If you're going to an evening event, however, and the invitation suggests "casual attire," that could mean an Almost a Suit ensemble, especially if the event is business-related. Again, if you're baffled, call in advance to make sure.

Perhaps the question that most often crops up in women's minds when decoding invitations is "What will everyone else be wearing?" That ques-tion can often be easily answered by picking up the phone and asking co-workers and business acquaintances. However, that can be a potential pitfall when everyone from your Clearly Casual company shows up in khakis and sweaters while employees of your host's Almost a Suit corpora-tion are wearing blazers and skirts. Remember that when attending a social function in a business capacity, you are not so much expressing yourself or your philosophy but rather representing your company or your business.

ALL ABOUT
PURSES

Shoes may walk the walk, but purses can talk the talk. Or so it seems.

For some mysterious reason, purses (aka handbags, pocketbooks, shoulder bags, clutches, etc.) have become the source of a semaphore-like language. By simply observing the quality and style of a purse, certain women can soak up volumes of information about the bag's owner. Never mind if the perceptions of these pocketbook psychics are accurate, the fact remains that, to many people, purses make an important statement, and thus should be chosen with care.

As usual, quality is a major consideration. You're not obliged to save up for an absolutely top-of-the-line designer logo model, but a well-made handbag or two is a good investment in your future.

Know, first, that leather is your friend. Synthetic bags made of "pleather" might be okay for a month or three, but the wear and tear of daily use will ultimately reveal their artificiality, making them look shoddy on your arm or wrist.

Second, remember that dark colors—black, brown, navy, burgundy— are de rigueur in the fall and winter seasons. They can also work year-round, although pale tones are acceptable—and refreshing—in the warmer months.

A PURSE SAMPLER
(Ranging loosely from dressiest to most casual)

Quilted bag with gold chain straps, black

Shoulder clutch, gray

Suede bag, bright red

Canvas/leather bag, pink

Tote with woven accent, brown and pink

Straw bag, red

Make sure that the purse you choose is the right size, shape, and style for your needs. Medium-sized clutches, handbags, or shoulder bags with metallic accents are natural choices for Almost a Suit ensembles. Leather bags, when accented by canvas or other fabrics, coordinate beautifully with Best of Both Worlds looks. Clearly Casual outfits can find their complements in relaxed totes—such as a leather and fabric weave for fall/winter and a bright straw "bucket" bag for the spring/fall season.

ALL ABOUT
CARRYALLS

Some women carry proper briefcases, with or without a shoulder strap. Some carry totes or book bags; other (usually younger) women transport their workday necessities in a backpack.

Whatever your style, it's a fact that lots of women end up carrying a portable office around with them, which may include a laptop computer, a cell phone, a datebook and/or electronic organizer, files, reports, and miscellaneous paperwork. According to a 1995 survey published as *Are You Normal?*, most women also carry reading material, makeup, an address book, and pain relievers in their business cases, while about a third of Americans also tote snacks, clothing, self-defense devices, and toothbrushes.

Before shopping for your ideal business case, take an honest inventory of the stuff you might need to stash on your worst day. Consider only those briefcases, totes, or carryalls that are large enough to accommodate your flotsam and jetsam without getting overstuffed; then narrow your choices to styles that harmonize with your business casual wardrobe.

Fine leather cases go best with Almost a Suit ensembles. This doesn't mean you have to carry a hard-shell attaché: Look for soft-sided pieces with stylish straps that are designed to house everything from laptops to lipsticks. For best results, choose real-leather colors like black and brown.

A CARRYALL SAMPLER
(Ranging loosely from dressiest to most casual)

Leather case with outer compartments and gold hardware, black

Suede tote, deep red with black trim, and gold-tone hardware

Canvas attaché, dark hunter green with leather accents

If you're a Best of Both Worlds woman, you might choose an expandable briefcase in flexible leather or a fabric with a comfy shoulder strap or transport your gear in a structured tote with finished edges and handles that means business. Word to the wise: Avoid carrying shapeless canvas totes, especially if they're emblazoned with logos or slogans.

Unlike their fancier sisters, Clearly Casual women can take advantage of tough carryalls made of industrial-strength fabrics. As a CC type, you might choose a bag that takes its design cues from intrepid campers (the backpack) or urban roughnecks (the messenger bag). If the carryall you crave is really untraditional in shape or form, you're smart to avoid loud colors and stick with dark or neutral tones.

ALL ABOUT
LUGGAGE

When you are traveling on business, your luggage is significant for two reasons. One, it has to accommodate all your essentials and keep them safe and unrumpled; two, the bags themselves become part of your ensemble and contribute to (or detract from) your overall professional image.

If you're a Clearly Casual gal and are traveling, say, to an island off the coast of Alaska to interview commercial fishermen, then style probably isn't your greatest concern. But for most women—no matter what their category of casual might be—it's smart to invest in luggage that suits their needs, looks good, and can take a beating.

Forget sliced bread; the greatest invention of the last century was the wheeled suitcase with the retractable handle. Wheels have had such an impact on the luggage industry that virtually all bags—no matter how big—are now designed to roll along conveniently behind you.

Look for bags that feature inline-skate-type wheels, which are quiet and easy to pull.

Before buying a piece of wheeled luggage, take it for a test drive to make sure that the handle length is comfortable for your height.

Most of today's baggage is covered in treated canvas or synthetic fabrics. The toughest synthetic is ballistic nylon, which is rated according to its "denier" (the thickness of the nylon). Checkable bags—which need to withstand plenty of punishment—should be 1,000 denier or more.

THE BASIC LUGGAGE WARDROBE
For Business Trips of Three to Four Days

Designed to comply with airline regulations, most wheeled carry-on bags are about 23 inches tall by 14 inches wide by 9 inches deep. Look for carry-ons with easy-access outside pockets and straps that can attach to or slide over the handles of larger wheeled pieces.

The typical business traveler needs only one wheeled check-through suitcase for short trips, but her choices vary. Medium-sized models measure about 26 inches tall by 17 inches wide by 12 inches deep. The next-largest standard is about 30 inches tall by 20 inches wide by 10.5 inches deep. A third option is the wheeled garment bag, ideal for carrying suits, coats, and other bulky items, and measuring about 20 inches tall by 22 inches wide by 10.5 inches deep.

It's always best to keep your business equipment separate from your personal items. To that end, choose an attaché, briefcase, or tote that can be attached to your carry-on luggage and is roomy enough to house your laptop, cell phone, paperwork, et cetera. To streamline your baggage, you might even consider using your business case as an ad hoc purse. It can store your wallet, datebook, and keys, while your more intimate necessities—lipstick, mirror, hairbrush—can be stashed in an outer pocket of your carry-on luggage.

WARNING: A NUMBER OF AIRLINES HAVE INTRODUCED NEW SIZE RESTRICTIONS FOR CARRY-ON BAGGAGE. BEFORE TRAVELING—OR BEFORE BUYING A PIECE OF LUGGAGE THAT CLAIMS TO ADHERE TO AIRLINE STANDARDS—CHECK WITH YOUR CARRIER OR TICKET AGENT TO MAKE SURE THE DIMENSIONS ARE ACCEPTABLE.

WHAT TO PACK FOR A
THREE-DAY BUSINESS TRIP

The problem with packing for business casual trips is that you don't really know how to dress until you get there—unless, of course, you've been there before. Assuming you haven't, the best fashion strategy is to plan a flexible wardrobe that might be a bit dressier than is really necessary *and* that definitely won't be too casual. After all, you don't want to be the only one in chinos and penny loafers in a sea of skirted suits and pumps.

The following packing template works fine for Almost a Suit and Best of Both Worlds archetypes. With a few adjustments, it can also serve as a guide for Clearly Casual travelers. If there is going to be a business-related but more social event, such as a celebration dinner or a cookout, call ahead to confirm the dress code.

Starting with a few well-chosen pieces that travel well, the business casual globe-trotter can create a number of outfits appropriate for a wide variety of situations. Here, a charcoal pantsuit and a long skirt combine with two shirts, two cardigans, one turtleneck sweater, and one scarf. Four different looks are achieved with a wardrobe small enough to fit into one carry-on suitcase.

WHAT YOU NEED

☐ One dark-colored pantsuit

☐ One blazer or jacket that coordinates with, but doesn't match, the suit trousers

☐ A skirt or a pair of pants that goes well with both jackets

☐ Three or four tops that can be worn with the above articles. Tops should cover many possibilities, from fairly formal (a long-sleeved white shirt or blouse) to relaxed (a colorful turtleneck jersey or cotton-knit tee).

☐ Three pairs of shoes—two to look good with your business outfits and the other to keep you comfortable while sprinting through airports or going on walking tours. Remember: Sneakers or athletic shoes are not considered acceptable for business travelers, especially in major cities or anywhere in Europe.

☐ Coordinating jewelry, belts, scarves, and hosiery

☐ Appropriate outerwear for the climate and the season and an umbrella if necessary

☐ The rest is up to you. Sleepwear, play clothes . . . what you wear outside of business is your business.

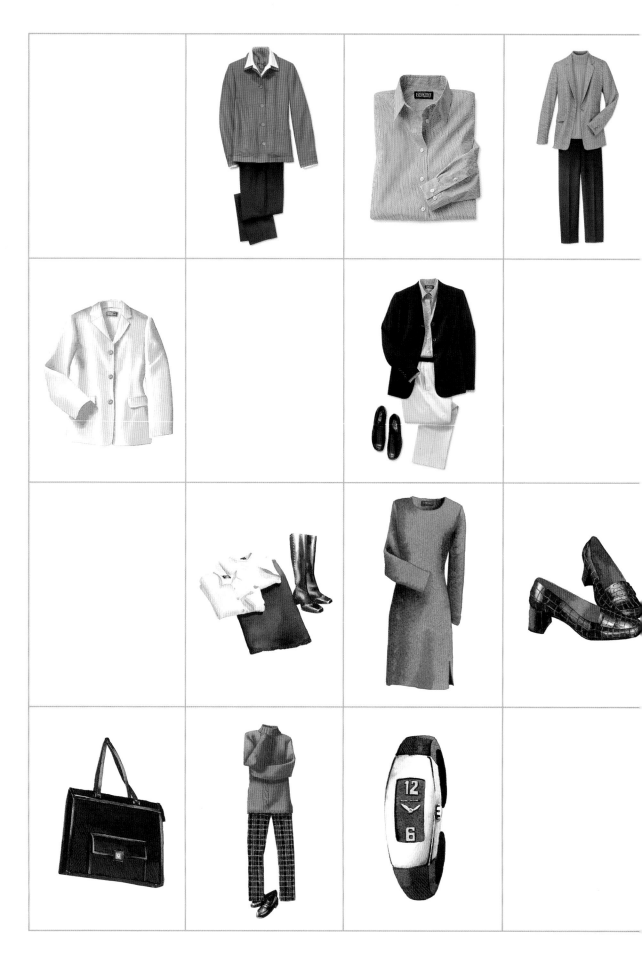

5

HOW TO FLATTER YOURSELF

FIVE

The subject, of course, is body types—

specifically, *your* body type, and how best to dress it in business casual fashions. The process begins with honest self-assessment. Chances are, you've been scrutinizing your body since you were a teenager and have been routinely accentuating your best features and downplaying your less-than-perfect areas. Even so, many women fall into a fashion rut and convince themselves that they absolutely can't wear this style or that. It's always a good idea to take a fresh look and discover the wardrobe pieces that make the most of what you've got.

See which of the symbols below best describe your shape. Then match your symbols to the following collection of outfits.

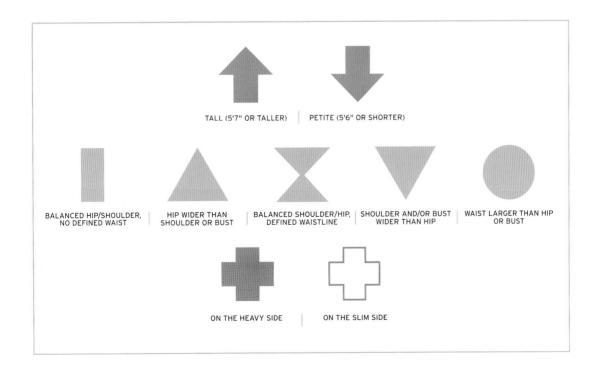

TALL (5'7" OR TALLER) | PETITE (5'6" OR SHORTER)

BALANCED HIP/SHOULDER, NO DEFINED WAIST | HIP WIDER THAN SHOULDER OR BUST | BALANCED SHOULDER/HIP, DEFINED WAISTLINE | SHOULDER AND/OR BUST WIDER THAN HIP | WAIST LARGER THAN HIP OR BUST

ON THE HEAVY SIDE | ON THE SLIM SIDE

ALMOST A SUIT ENSEMBLES

Suit, with three-button blazer and pleated pants, light tan; fine-gauge sweater, untucked, red

Gabardine suit, with three-button blazer and flat-front pants, navy; oxford shirt, pink

Gabardine suit, with single-button blazer and flat-front pants, olive; pinpoint broadcloth shirt, white; pumps, black

Tropical-weight-wool suit, with two-button blazer and pleated pants, glen plaid; belt, black; broadcloth shirt, blue; pumps, black

BEST OF BOTH WORLDS
BLENDINGS

Three-button cashmere-blend blazer, winter white; flat-front wool pants, charcoal; mock turtleneck, charcoal

Blazer, navy; pleated chinos, cream; belt, black; long-sleeved cotton broadcloth shirt, pink; shoes, black

Single-button linen blazer, flax; slim leg side-zip chinos, light stone; short-sleeved V-neck T-shirt, white; twill sandals, light khaki

Stretch-knit long cardigan, black; stretch-knit, elastic-waist long skirt, black; Supima cotton T-shirt, ivory; strap skimmers, black

CLEARLY CASUAL COMBOS

Cotton cowl-neck sweater, gray; stretch-knit pants, light gray

Plaid broadcloth shirt, light green; cashmere cardigan, pale orange; natural-fit jeans, light stone; web belt, black; loafer mules, black

Cable fine-gauge cotton crewneck sweater, navy; cropped chinos, light stone; canvas sneaker-style shoes, yellow; web belt, yellow; small canvas tote, yellow-trimmed

Supima cotton T-shirt, light blue; flat-front chinos, light stone; driving moccasins, tan

KNOW THINE ENEMIES

If you have a large bust, avoid wrap-front tops, and beware of shirts and blouses that button down the front. Make sure they're roomy and don't gap at the bust, and err on the side of caution when deciding how far down to unbutton.

If you're overweight or out of shape, don't emphasize your trouble spots, and avoid outfits that cinch or cling. If you want to minimize your waistline, for instance, try combining pants with an untucked jersey and a jacket, a long sweater, or an overshirt. Go for more flowing fits but don't try to hide behind overly baggy clothes.

Heavy-legged women often do better in dresses and skirts than in trousers. If you do wear pants, choose styles that are wide from hip to ankle.

Those of you who are especially tall or lanky need to be sure that shirt cuffs and jacket cuffs extend right to the wrist bone, and that trouser legs are exactly as long as they need to be—and not a millimeter shorter.

The long and short of it refers to more than height. Tall women can be short-waisted and short women can be long-waisted. Look carefully at the length of your torso and where your waist is. When choosing a suit, remember that Chanel-style, waist-length, or bolero-style jackets are more flattering to short-waisted women, while those longer in the torso should look for jackets that are closer to fingertip-length.

If you have a bit of an abdomen (editor and style maven Helen Gurley Brown refers to hers as a "poochie"), watch out for high-waisted, trouser-style pleated pants or skirts that can accentuate any bulge below the waist. Flat-front, side-zip pants and skirts with no waistband or a waistband that lies just below or on the belly button can be more flattering—but always make sure your top is long enough to prevent any skin from peeking through!

Even the thin can be thick-waisted. If you have narrow hips but don't have a pronounced waistline, try belts or contrasts between top and bottom to create the illusion of a waist. Those who are heavier and thick-waisted will do better with longer tops and a tone-on-tone or monochrome palette, which draws the eye up and down rather than side-to-side.

When shopping for trousers, pay close attention to fit. Make sure they aren't tight at the waist or torso and don't pull or bunch up in the crotch area. On-seam pockets should lie flat against the contour of your hips. If they stick out, try another size or choose pants with horizontal L-shaped pockets, discreet besom pockets (with welted slits), or no pockets at all.

Pleats can be found on tailored trousers as well as casual pants such as chinos. You can opt for double-pleat or single-pleat models; in either case, the creases should fall in a straight line from the waist to the ankles. If the pleats gape or spread, you need a larger size or a different style.

THE PROPER FIT

The most expensive and elegant ensembles won't do anything for you if they don't fit you well. Ill-fitting clothes are not only unflattering to your figure, but they can also make a person look unkempt or poorly groomed.

Clothes that don't fit well are available in astonishing varieties. An all-around review in a three-way mirror can speak volumes.

Start with pants: Are they visibly tight in the crotch or rear? Do the pleats pull or flatten out on your thighs? Does the waistband gap at the back? Are the pants too short (exposing your ankle), or too long (hanging almost to the floor)? If so, get them altered, or try another size or style.

Next, let's look at blazers and jackets. A well-fitting blazer follows the natural lines of the body and is not tight in the hips and loose in the waist or vice versa, doesn't buckle or pull at the buttons or back vents, has sleeves that end on or just beyond the wrist bone, and fits the shoulders and armpits well enough that you can raise your hand comfortably.

When it comes to blouses, shirts, and cardigan sweaters, the most important rule is this: There must be a button closure positioned at the widest part of your bust (usually directly between the crest of your breasts). Otherwise, your blouse, shirt, or cardigan will never look right. Shoulders and sleeves are significant, too.

Skirts shouldn't cling tightly to your rump or thighs, nor should waistbands be so snug that they cause "midriff bulge" above or below. Also, beware of slits; a perfectly modest skirt with an innocent-looking slit up the front or side may expose every inch of your leg once you sit down.

Decades ago, an anonymous fashionista remarked that one's clothes "should fit well enough to show you're a woman but loose enough to show you're a lady." The sentiment is old-fashioned and the language is outdated, but the advice still makes sense, even after all these years.

WHAT'S YOUR SIZE?

	X-SMALL		SMALL		MEDIUM		LARGE		X-LARGE	
	2	4	6	8	10	12	14	16	18	20
BUST	32	33	34	35	36	37 ½	39	40 ½	42 ½	44 ½
WAIST	24	25	26	27	28	29 ½	31	32 ½	34 ½	36 ½
HIP	34 ½	35 ½	36 ½	37 ½	38 ½	40	41 ½	43	45	47
RISE (petite)	24	24 ¾	25 ½	26 ¼	27	27 ¾	28 ½	29 ¼	30	–
RISE (regular)	–	25 ¾	26 ½	27 ¼	28	28 ¾	29 ½	30 ¼	31	31 ¾
RISE (tall)	–	–	–	28 ¼	29	29 ¾	30 ½	31 ¼	32	32 ¾
ARM (petite)	28 ⅛	28 ½	28 ⅞	29 ¼	29 ⅝	30	30 ⅜	30 ¾	31 ⅛	–
ARM (regular)	–	29 ¾	30 ⅛	30 ½	30 ⅞	31 ¼	31 ⅝	32	32 ⅜	32 ¾
ARM (tall)	–	–	–	31 ½	31 ⅞	32 ¼	32 ⅝	33	33 ⅜	33 ¾

	1X		2X		3X	
	16W	18W	20W	22W	24W	26W
BUST	42 ½	44 ½	46 ½	48 ½	50 ½	52 ½
WAIST	34 ½	36 ½	38 ½	40 ½	42 ½	44 ½
HIP	45	47	49	51	53	55
RISE (petite)						
RISE (regular)	29 ¾	30 ½	31 ¼	32	32 ¾	33 ½
RISE (tall)						
ARM (petite)						
ARM (regular)	31 ¾	32 ⅛	32 ½	32 ⅞	33 ⅛	33 ⅜
ARM (tall)						

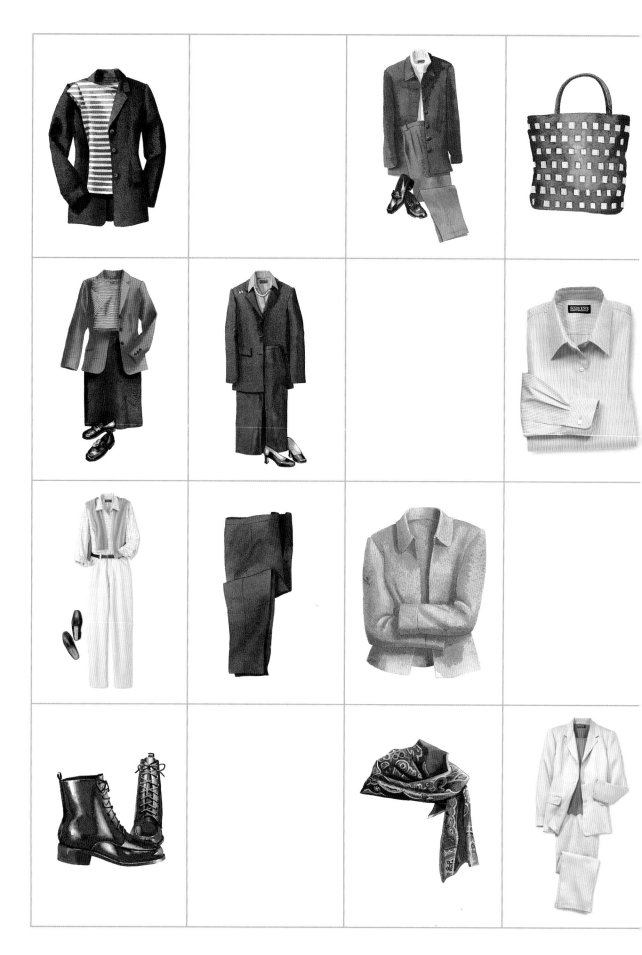

6

CARING FOR YOUR GARMENTS

HOW TO GET THE BEST RETURN ON YOUR WARDROBE INVESTMENT

Good clothes deserve tender loving care.

There's an art to keeping your wardrobe in tip-top condition, and taking the time to do so will repay you richly. "Keeping your clothes well pressed will keep you from looking hard-pressed," quipped Coleman Cox. But padded ironing boards and proper steam settings are but a small part of business casual wardrobe maintenance. A number of casual basics call for machine- or hand-washing with special care instructions. If your time is limited, and you're tempted to drop off a pile of clothes to your friendly neighborhood dry cleaner, think again: Although dry-cleaning is convenient and effective, you can also get good results at home.

Like it or not, the future of your closet is in your hands.

Ready to accept the challenge? Read on.

PANTS

CLEANING

✳ Pants made of wool, most wool blends, linen, and rayon gabardine must be professionally dry-cleaned, and it should be done once or twice a year.

✳ Some trousers are made from washable wool, but check the label and be absolutely positive before attempting to launder them.

✳ Fine wool garments should be brushed after each wearing with a soft but firm-bristled brush. This will remove the dust that collects between the fibers of the fabric.

✳ Pants made of cotton, cotton-poly blends, or denim—including chinos, poplins, and twills—may be machine-washed and tumbled dry on a low setting or line-dried. Use a warm iron if needed. As always, check the label.

✳ Corduroy pants should be turned inside out before laundering.

✳ Many microfiber slacks require dry-cleaning, but some blends are machine washable. Whether the label calls for it or not, a gentle cycle is advised. If tumble drying is allowed, do it on a cool setting and be extra careful not to overdry.

PRESSING

✳ To spruce up creased trousers, you will need a press cloth (a cotton kitchen towel will do) and a spray water bottle or steam iron. Spritz the area to be pressed, cover it with the cloth, and press—one leg at a time, please—using the appropriate fabric setting on your iron.

HANGING

✳ Remove the belt from the trousers and empty the pockets. Crease at the center front and center back and hang the pants from the bottom hem on a hanger that's specially made for trousers.

BLAZERS AND JACKETS

CLEANING

✳ Jackets and blazers need to be professionally dry-cleaned, but don't do it more than once or twice a year. Between wearings, brush your jackets—pockets emptied, buttons undone—with a soft-bristled yet fairly stiff brush. Use short, quick strokes, first upward and then down.

✳ If your blazer or jacket becomes rumpled, hang it in the bathroom while you're taking a shower, and let it steam for ten minutes or so.

HANGING

✳ After each wearing, hang your jacket on a contoured hanger and let it rest, unbuttoned and pockets emptied, for at least twenty-four hours before wearing it again.

STORING

✳ Don't hang jackets or blazers in plastic bags. Instead, use shoulder covers or cloth bags, which will protect the fabric from dust while still allowing it to "breathe."

✳ High-quality wool jackets should be cleaned and put in a cedar closet or in cold storage off season; otherwise, they may fall victim to moths.

SHIRTS

CLEANING

✳ Shirts made of cotton can be machine-washed and -dried. Be sure to remove the shirts from the dryer before they're 100 percent dry.

✳ Silk is highly absorbent, so soiled silk shirts need to be washed promptly. Dry-cleaning or hand-washing is usually called for, but some silks are machine-washable. In any case, silks should be line-dried.

✳ Rayon garments are, for the most part, dry-clean-only. If you do own a washable rayon shirt, it should be hand-washed and drip-dried from a wood or padded hanger.

✳ Most linens must be hand-washed, though some are machine-washable. In either case, avoid the dryer and drip-dry the shirt from a wood or padded hanger.

PRESSING

✳ Keep cotton shirts damp until you're ready to press them by spritzing them thoroughly with water and rolling them tightly in a bath towel. Use a warm to hot iron for 100 percent cottons, and a slightly lower setting for cotton blends. Don't press over the buttons, as this tends to cause breakage. Alternatively, hang the blouse and use a hand steamer.

✳ Silk and rayon garments are sensitive to heat; press them on cooler settings.

✳ Linen should not be pressed bone-dry. Moisten the fabric with a spritz of water before pressing.

SWEATERS AND KNITS

CLEANING

✳ Most sweaters should either be hand-washed in cold water or professionally dry-cleaned, depending on the manufacturer's recommendations.

✳ Many cotton-knit sweaters are machine-washable. For best results, turn the sweater inside out, wash using the delicate cycle, then tumble dry on a low setting.

HAND-WASHING

✳ Use cold water and a mild soap that's recommended for wool or silk knits.

✳ Turn the sweater inside out and work the soapy water gently through the sweater, without twisting or stretching.

✳ Rinse the sweater in cold tap water.

✳ Repeat the process.

✳ Gently squeeze out excess water, then lay the sweater across a large terry-cloth towel.

✳ Roll the sweater in the towel and pat it.

✳ Place the sweater faceup on a dry towel and "block" it; that is, reshape it by hand into its original proportions.

MAINTENANCE

✳ Between wearings, shake out your sweater and let it air out by laying it flat on a cotton towel, away from direct sunlight.

✳ If your sweater develops "pills," gently razor them off. Don't attempt to pull at them, as this will damage the weave.

✳ If your sweater develops wrinkles or creases, hold a steam iron over—not on—the affected areas.

STORAGE

✳ Never hang a sweater. Instead, lay it flat in a cool, dry place.

✳ Sweaters should not be wrapped in plastic, as this will trap moisture. Natural, breathable storage boxes are a better bet.

✳ In the off-season, wool sweaters should be stored with mothballs or cedar chips.

BELTS

✳ Fabric belts can be spruced up using a good spot cleaner.

✳ On leather belts, remove minor nicks and scratches with shoe polish. Buff them well afterward, so that the polish doesn't seep into the waistband of your pants or skirt.

✳ Blemishes on suede or nubuck can be buffed out with a soft cloth.

SHOES

If you've invested in a pair of high-quality shoes, resist the urge to wear them right away. Instead, take them to a shoemaker and request that he apply a thin rubber half sole and heel to the shoes' bottoms. Your footwear will last much longer, and you'll avoid slipping on brand-new leather soles.

CLEANING

✷ Fabric shoes can be spot-cleaned using a mild detergent and a soft brush. Rinse with warm water, pat with a towel, then air-dry.

✷ Leather shoes may be brushed with a horsehair brush and cleaned with saddle soap, which also conditions and preserves leather. Do not use saddle soap on oil-tanned leather.

✷ Suede shoes are usually brushed—cleaned with short, quick strokes. Some spots can be removed using an art gum eraser; if the suede is scarred, however, try gently removing the marks with fine sandpaper.

POLISHING

✷ Before polishing leather shoes, clean them with saddle soap: Apply a small amount of cream polish to a soft cloth. Using circular motions, rub the cream into the leather, beginning at the toes. Fold up the cloth and buff each shoe. Shine with a clean, soft cloth.

STORAGE AND MAINTENANCE

✷ Use a shoehorn when you put on shoes.

✷ Store shoes in shoe trees to help maintain their shape.

✷ If suede shoes get wet, stuff them with newspaper until they're thoroughly dry.

✷ Rotate your shoe wardrobe. Wearing the same pair day in and day out doesn't give the leather a chance to breathe properly.

✷ When traveling, pack your shoes in shoe bags.

SCARVES

✷ Delicate silk or silk-blend scarves should be hand-washed or spot-cleaned.

✷ Wool, cashmere, and pashmina scarves last longest when they're dry-cleaned. Not too often, though.

Someday, what you wear won't matter.

Your success will be a direct result of your talent, intelligence, spirit, dedication, and good ideas. You'll make the rules. Others won't argue.

Until then, it is our wish that you give yourself the gift of dressing smart. The right outfits won't guarantee a prepaid ticket to the top, but they will help smooth the road you're traveling on. Doors won't automatically open just because you're wearing great shoes and a beautiful blazer, but they won't automatically close, either.

Whether you're balancing books, managing a department, running a company, or putting together a wardrobe that takes you from board meetings to construction sites, smart is smart—and it shows.

In this ever-changing world, there are few things that we really have control over. Clothing is one of them. So, seize your style. Conquer your closet. Make fashion a slave to you. Go forth and prosper, and do it all in casual comfort.

INDEX

ABOUT LANDS' END

Lands' End is a direct merchant of classically inspired clothing and home products offered through specialty catalogs, on the Internet, and in Sears stores. Celebrating its fortieth anniversary in 2003, Lands' End is world renowned for its customer service and "Guaranteed. Period.®" approach to customer satisfaction. For more information about Lands' End, visit www.landsend.com.

ABOUT THE AUTHOR

Todd Lyon is an artist-turned-writer who has authored or coauthored more than a dozen books focused on fashion, food, business, and fun, including *Chic Simple: Cooking, The Domain Book of Intuitive Home Design, The New Year's Eve Compendium, The Intuitive Businesswoman,* and *How to Buy Your Perfect Wedding Dress.* Her articles and essays have appeared in the *New York Times* and the *Boston Globe,* as well as in *Cosmopolitan, Biography, Saveur,* and *Bust* magazines; currently, she is a columnist for the *New Haven Register,* her hometown paper.